"A foam roller for your faith! Five to ten minutes of this devotional will leave you rejuvenated as you discover the unique connection between running and faith. Packed with entertaining stories, practical running tips, and challenging faith steps, this book is the ultimate training tool."

—CJ Albertson, college coach, indoor marathon world record holder; Chelsey Albertson, U.S. Olympic marathon trials qualifier

"Having known the Youngs for over twenty years, I've observed the anvil on which these amazing devotionals were forged. Using personal examples and practical suggestions, they apply Bible verses to life and running, showing us vividly how to 'walk, run, and soar' spiritually and physically."

—John Volkman, has run a marathon in all 50 states and 10 provinces, and has coached marathon runners for over 20 years

"This book is the perfect amount of storytelling, devotion, and practical running advice; such a gift from an inspiring couple! I also love that it gives me an opportunity to journal and record both my spiritual and running journey at the same time."

—Sunny Arada, owner and founder of Endure Jewelry and former NCAA Division I track athlete

"Dorina is an encourager who moves women forward in their faith. Her words will give you the courage to take the next brave, Jesus-following step in your story."

—Holley Gerth, *Wall Street Journal* bestselling author of *You're Already Amazing*

"Biblical resources for spiritual perspectives to inspire and instruct my athletes. Dorina and Shawn have created a powerful and applicable guide-book of higher purpose for runners of the faith, and I know I will use it for years to come in countless circumstances."

—Ray Winter, PhD, cross-country and track-and-field head coach, Fresno Pacific University

WALK, RUN, SOAR

WALK, RUN, SOAR

A 52-Week Running Devotional

Dorina Gilmore Young

with Shawn Young

BETHANYHOUSE
a division of Baker Publishing Group
Minneapolis, Minnesota

Published by Bethany House Publishers
11400 Hampshire Avenue South
Bloomington, Minnesota 55438
www.bethanyhouse.com

Bethany House Publishers is a division of
Baker Publishing Group, Grand Rapids, Michigan

ISBN 978-0-7642-3605-1 (trade paper)
ISBN 978-0-7642-3830-7 (casebound)

Cover design by Kara Klontz

Author represented by Books & Such Literary Management

CONTENTS

Foreword   9

Introduction   11

1. Cultivating Courage   15

2. Beauty from Ashes   19

3. Walking with Purpose   23

4. He Refreshes My Soul   27

5. Your Pace Is Your Pace   31

6. Cloud of Witnesses   35

7. Hydrating Well   39

8. Running Away from the Lies   43

9. Seasoned with Salt   47

10. Running through Life's Hurdles   51

11. Press On toward the Goal   55

12. Trust Your Coach   59

13. Get Up and Walk   63

14. Learning to Breathe   67

15. Looking beyond the Haze   71

16. Perfect Practice Makes Perfect   75

17. The Power of Suggestion   79

18. Traversing Life's Trails   83

19. Building Spiritual Muscles   88

20. Showing Up Matters   92

21. Coming Full Circle   96

22. Soaring through the Clouds   100

23. Walking on Water   104

24. Loving Your Neighbor on the Trail   108

25. Friend and Forerunner   112

26. Running for Diamonds   116

27. Suiting Up with Proper Gear 120

28. Valuing the Building Process 124

29. Battling Fear on the Course 128

30. Honoring Our Sacred Bodies 132

31. Your Race Isn't Over Yet 136

32. Walking Like Jesus 140

33. Letting God Nourish Us 144

34. Hitting the Wall 148

35. Under His Wings 152

36. Running to Worship 156

37. Training Together 160

38. Following My Coach 164

39. Resting in Unforced Rhythms 168

40. Running toward the Rock 172

41. Developing Mental Toughness 176

42. Building Muscle Memory 180

43. Run Like a Girl 184

44. Learning from the Crepe Myrtle 188

45. Running against the Wind 192

46. Fighting the Good Fight 196

47. Praying While Running 200

48. Navigating Injuries 204

49. Resting as Part of Training 208

50. Dealing with Disappointment 212

51. Finishing Well 216

52. Running the Ultramarathon 219

Appendix 1: How to Form a Running Group 225
Appendix 2: Warm-up Drills for Runners 232
Appendix 3: Walk, Run, Soar 5K 238
Appendix 4: Walk, Run, Soar 10K 241
Appendix 5: Walk, Run, Soar Half Marathon 244
Appendix 6: Walk, Run, Soar Weekly Mileage Chart 247
Appendix 7: Walk, Run, Soar Annual Mileage Chart 248
Acknowledgments 249
Notes 255

FOREWORD

When I look back at my career, it wasn't the two Olympic Games I had the honor of competing in, or the American record I set in the half marathon, or even running 2:04 at the 2011 Boston Marathon that I treasure the most. Rather, it is a still, quiet moment when I was thirteen years old, before any running ever began, when I was looking out the window at the sparkling blue waters in Big Bear Lake, California, that I cherish most. This was the moment when I encountered God for the first time in a still, small, quiet inner voice challenging me to run around the lake. It would have been easy for me to dismiss this feeling as a passing random urge to do something that I always hated to do (run), but there was something about it that captured me. It captured me in a way that made it impossible to let it go. This small encounter with God changed the trajectory of my life forever.

The following Saturday I laced up my running shoes with my dad and embarked on what had to be the world's longest, slowest, most painful run in history (at least that's how it felt to me). When I finally stumbled through the door and collapsed on the couch, I felt like I heard God speak to me again that one day I would run with the best guys in the world, and that I had been given that gift to help and love other people. I would spend the next twenty years of my running career pursuing this vision, beginning a wonderful journey full of exhilarating highs, gut-wrenching lows, and everything in between, experiencing God at deeper levels with each passing stride.

In the same way that I experienced God so deeply throughout my running career, I believe He wants you to experience Him in new and deeper ways through your running. Something that has always bothered me about sports is that usually there is only one winner. Only one person gets to stand on top of the podium and say "I did it!" while everyone else is left with the emptiness of not achieving that top step. But this isn't the case with God. Knowing and experiencing Him truly is sweeter than anything anyone could ever achieve—more than any gold medal, world record, or goal reached. He is sweeter. He is true satisfaction. And the good news is that we can all have Him, all at the same time, and have as much of Him as we want. Which leads to the next question that is probably running through your mind: How?

We all need guides in life. Guides come in many different forms: family members, friends, pastors, teammates, messages, and books to name a few. The book you are holding in your hand is one such powerful guide to help you experience God every step of your journey. It will turn your attention away from the lesser goals and toward the greatest goal: experiencing God on the run. My prayer for you is that you will have an experience similar to my own: one that was full of amazing experiences, people, and performances, but most important, encounters with God that mark you for the rest of your days.

—Ryan Hall, Olympian, author, coach, speaker

INTRODUCTION

Hey, friend! If you are a walker or a runner who has a hunch that running and faith are intricately connected, you're in the right place.

If you're a runner who wants to accomplish your physical goals, but also longs for a more personal connection with God, then we need to chat.

If you're a runner who deep down wants your training to engage the body, mind, soul, and spirit, this book is for you.

If you have ever felt out of breath or stuck in life, I am here to help you find new strength to press on. I can certainly relate. After my husband, Ericlee, died from cancer in 2014, I wasn't sure if I could ever run again. He had been my coach, my running partner, and my biggest cheerleader for almost a dozen years. He trained me for my first half marathon and then my first marathon. He logged hundreds of miles with me, pushing our daughters in the jogging stroller and pushing me to personal records.

I still remember that first week after my husband's death when I ventured out to the track for a workout. I wasn't sure I could run without him. I laced up my running shoes and took a deep breath. I ran once around the oval and then began to hear it. Ericlee's coaching voice boomed from heaven. He was telling me to lift my knees, to steady my breathing, to square my shoulders, and run. My eyes, body, and heart were lifted from grief to hope.

The prophet Isaiah says, "But those who hope in the LORD will renew their strength. They will soar on wings like eagles; they will run and not grow weary, they will walk and not be faint" (Isaiah 40:31). These words remind us that we are called to place our hope in Him. We cannot trust in our own sense of control and purpose. He is the One who can help us begin to walk and run again after crippling life circumstances.

Different versions of the Bible use different words like *wait* (ESV), *trust* (NLT), and *wait upon* (MSG) in place of *hope*. These words help deepen our understanding of this passage. When we have that hope and wait upon God, He leads us in surprising ways to fly like eagles.

Eagles are beautiful, majestic birds created by God to soar. They have long, large wings. Their bodies are very light with bones that are hollow. Their skeletons weigh only about half a pound, but their wings are very strong. When eagles fly, they flap their wings for only a short time to gain altitude. Then they stretch their wings horizontally and use wind thermals to soar or glide through the air, conserving energy.

A wind thermal is a big gust of wind that rises up from the atmosphere. Eagles wait and perch (sometimes for days) before they catch a good, strong wind thermal to carry them to where they want to go. Like the eagle, we also must "wait with hope," listening for the Holy Spirit to whisper, nudge, or direct us where to run next.

While we wait, Isaiah 40 says He "renews our strength." An eagle molts, which is the natural way God replenishes its wings. Similarly, God can give us a dose of renewed strength, power, and ability while we are waiting or putting in the miles training for a race. We can't simply rely on our own human strength because it is too-often misguided and will eventually run out. Like the eagle, we need to conserve energy and soar on the wind the Holy Spirit provides.

My heart is to run alongside you this year and help coach you to connect with God, develop muscle memory, and catch a second wind to soar to the finish line. Whether you are a walker or a seasoned runner, this book was designed with you in mind.

In this 52-week experience, I encourage you to read one devotional at the start of each week, and then spend time journaling and taking the faith steps throughout your week. You don't have to start at the beginning of the year. Whether it's January, June, or November, just jump in today!

If you're a runner or walker, my husband, Shawn, has included coaching tips to help you improve your training and your form. You might couple these weekly tips with some of the workout plans for 5K, 10K, or half-marathon distances included in the appendix. We also have included space at the end of each chapter for writing your reflections and recording details about your workouts.

This book lends itself well to meeting with other runners and walkers. You might connect with a friend for accountability or form a running group or team to share these weekly reflections together. Discuss the questions, memorize the Scriptures, and cheer each other on to your personal finish lines.

Friend, when you reach the final page of this devotional journal, my hope and prayer is that you will *walk*, *run*, and *soar* knowing that Jesus is with you every step of the way.

1

CULTIVATING COURAGE

Have I not commanded you? Be strong and courageous. Do not be afraid; do not be discouraged, for the LORD your God will be with you wherever you go.

Joshua 1:9

FAITH FUEL

I still remember the night before I ran my first half marathon. Butterflies danced in my stomach. Even though I had trained hard and followed the plan my coach put together for me, I was still nervous. *Would all those practice runs really pay off? Did I drink enough water? Would my knees hold up? Would I make it to the finish line?* All these questions crowded my mind.

I also vividly remember the night before running my first full marathon, which was in San Diego. Again, I put in the time and persevered through the long runs and strength workouts, but I had to battle the fears floating through my heart. The 26.2 miles felt daunting. I woke up several times that night, wondering if I was really ready for the race. With trembling legs, I prayed for courage for the next morning to get on that starting line.

In the book of Joshua, God encourages Joshua to "be strong and courageous." Joshua served Moses during Israel's forty years of wandering in the wilderness. Joshua was a faithful servant and proved a worthy leader whom God intended to use to lead the Israelites into the promised land after Moses' death. First, God prepares Joshua's heart and urges him to prepare the people.

As He is calling Joshua up to leadership, God imparts courage to him. He commands him three times in Joshua 1:5–9 to "be strong and courageous." That repetition is like a holy highlighter emphasizing the importance of courage to Joshua. That word *courage* is used throughout the Old Testament, meaning to "be brave," "keep hold of," "make firm," "grow strong," and "be swift-footed." Courage also means "breath" in Hebrew. Reciprocally, when we are discouraged, we are short of breath.

God follows up His command to Joshua with these words of assurance: "Do not be afraid; do not be discouraged, for the LORD your God will be with you wherever you go" (Joshua 1:9). God isn't asking Joshua to muster up a bunch of courage on his own. He's not asking him to pull up his proverbial bootstraps and prove himself a courageous warrior. He's simply reminding Joshua that courage comes in knowing God will be with Him. He gifts Joshua with His presence.

Sometimes in life, courage is standing at the intersection of fear and faith, and choosing faith. Sometimes courage is humbly admitting our weaknesses and moving forward. Sometimes courage means venturing out to run a distance we have never run before. And sometimes courage means getting back up after a horrible race and training again.

Friend, let God breathe courage into you today. If He can get me to the finish line of that first half marathon and marathon, He will surely go with you as you run, walk, and maybe even soar through your race. "Above all, be strong and very courageous" (Joshua 1:7 HCSB).

FAITH STEP: Sometimes it helps when we are running or walking to repeat a phrase to ourselves. Make "be strong and courageous" your mantra for this week. Run and feel the strength and rhythm of these words in your heart.

INSPIRATION: "Being brave, for me, means not giving up on the things that make me feel alive."

 —GABE GRUNEWALD, 2014 USA indoor track-and-field 3,000m champion; battled cancer from 2009–2019

NOTES FROM COACH SHAWN: In a race, spend some time mentally chanting a positive phrase or song lyric that will help keep you focused, relaxed, and running on a good rhythm. One suggestion is to use "Walk, run, soar."

Use the space below to jot down some notes about your daily workouts or goals.

SUNDAY   MILES

MONDAY   MILES

TUESDAY   MILES

WEDNESDAY   MILES

THURSDAY   MILES _____

FRIDAY   MILES _____

SATURDAY   MILES _____

TOTAL MILES _____

2

BEAUTY FROM ASHES

The Spirit of the Sovereign LORD is on me . . . to comfort all who mourn, and provide for those who grieve in Zion—to bestow on them a crown of beauty instead of ashes, the oil of joy instead of mourning, and a garment of praise instead of a spirit of despair.

Isaiah 61:1, 2–3

FAITH FUEL

My friends and I rolled out of camp bunk beds early. The air was brisk but the sun greeted us with a promise of warmth. I joined my running buddies at the starting line for another attempt at the Shadow of the Giants trail race.

"Three, two, one, go!" the race director bellowed, his voice echoing through the forest. And we were off.

My lungs burned as we headed uphill through the grove of Sequoia trees at 5,000-feet elevation. Inhale. Lift. Exhale. Lift. Inhale. Lift. I tried to find the rhythm of my breath and feet to make it up that first long hill. I had confidence, knowing I had completed this race before, but five miles of hills is still five miles of hills. I knew what to expect, but I still had to put in the work.

This time, as I ran the Shadow of the Giants race, I couldn't help but notice the landscape. The trail through the Nelder Grove—near Yosemite National Park—looked strikingly different from the year before when I ran the same race. Fallen trees and blackened trunks provided a striking stark contrast against the backdrop of the bright blue sky.

A wildfire earlier in the year blazed its way through 12,407 acres of this forest. The cause of the fire was unknown, but it threatened communities, historic buildings, resorts, and the Yosemite Mountain Sugar Pine Railroad.

When a fire rages through dry underbrush, it clears thick growth so nourishing sunlight can reach the forest floor. This encourages the growth of native species. Where forest fires destroy, new life always springs up. A resilient tree that survives the fire can even experience a growth spurt.

As I ran, I noticed evidence of new growth. Green grass and leaves sprouted in all directions. Wildflowers dotted the trail. As I rounded the corner after the steepest part of the race, angled light beamed through the blackened tree trunks. Beauty rose from the ashes.

Out of my family's grief, a fierce sense of hope has risen in my life these last several years. I still bear the scars of loss, but God uses these to open doors so I can encourage others. My three daughters have resilient spirits, which I believe spring from the fire they have walked through. Sometimes life is about breathing and lifting, moving forward one step at a time. Our hearts were singed, but we have found unexpected joy in the journey.

Do you feel like you are running uphill through the dark? Do you feel the sear of the fire at your heels? It's taken more than a few runs to learn that the challenge is in how I respond. Will we let life's fires destroy us or refine us? Will we sit in the ashes or will we wear a crown of beauty?

FAITH STEP: What is a difficult circumstance you are facing? Write out a prayer responding with hope.

INSPIRATION: "Sometimes you have to go through the tragedy before you can experience the jubilation of the triumph, and so I was super proud with the way that he was able to find that gear."

—COACH ED EYESTONE on his athlete winning the men's NCAA 10,000m championship in 2019

NOTES FROM COACH SHAWN: If you begin to struggle during a long run or race, try consuming fifty to a hundred calories either from food (gels, chews, etc.) or from a running beverage. The sustenance may perk you up and give you a second wind.

Use the space below to jot down some notes about your daily workouts or goals.

SUNDAY   MILES

MONDAY   MILES

TUESDAY   MILES

WEDNESDAY   MILES

THURSDAY   MILES

FRIDAY   MILES_____

SATURDAY   MILES_____

                                          TOTAL MILES_____

3

WALKING WITH PURPOSE

In light of all this, here's what I want you to do. While I'm locked up here, a prisoner for the Master, I want you to get out there and walk—better yet, run!—on the road God called you to travel. I don't want any of you sitting around on your hands. I don't want anyone strolling off, down some path that goes nowhere.

Ephesians 4:1 MSG

FAITH FUEL

When I first started dating my husband, Shawn, I noticed he had this quirky habit of deliberately swinging his arms wherever he walked. Whether he was walking through the grocery store or strolling down the street, he would bend his elbows at a 90-degree angle and swing his arms like he did when he was running. One day I teased him about it.

He simply answered, "I'm practicing my arm form."

As we began to coach marathon and cross-country teams together, I often heard him reiterate his philosophy of "walking with purpose." He encouraged the athletes to practice proper arm form wherever they went. Some of our kids couldn't run the whole cross-country course at first, so he urged them to swing their arms and walk with purpose even when they were tired. This posture helped propel them to the finish line.

According to the dictionary, to *walk* means "to advance or travel on foot at a moderate speed or pace." In a spiritual sense, walking with God means to abide with Him, obey His commands, and keep a deliberate pace, following His lead.

Adam and Eve hear God walking in the garden in Genesis 3:8. This very deliberate description of God walking tells us something about our heavenly Father. He simply wants to walk with us. I'm always astounded that our all-powerful, all-knowing God, who is everywhere, longs for personal connection with His children. There is an intimacy and intentionality in walking together, shoulder-to-shoulder.

Throughout the Old Testament, we read accounts of people of faith-walking with God. In Genesis 5, we learn that Enoch lived a total of 365 years *walking* with His heavenly Father. "Enoch walked faithfully with God; then he was no more, because God took him away" (Genesis 5:24).

In Genesis 6:9, we read about Noah *walking* with God: "Noah was a righteous man, blameless among the people of his time, and he walked faithfully with God." God was Noah's pacer and gave Him assurance as he built the ark with no sign of rain on the horizon.

In the same way, Abraham and Isaac were characterized as men who *walked* with God. When Israel is giving Joseph and his sons his blessing before he dies, he says this: "May the God before whom my fathers Abraham and Isaac walked faithfully, the God who has been my shepherd all my life to this day, the Angel who has delivered me from all harm —may he bless these boys" (Genesis 48:15–16). Israel's desire is for his grandsons to walk with God in the same way their fathers and forefathers did.

Paul urges the church of Ephesus and all of us to walk with purpose in a manner worthy of the calling God has given us. Paul writes with passion from prison about this: "I want you to get out there and walk—better yet, run!—on the road God called you to travel. I don't want any of you sitting around on your hands. I don't want anyone strolling off, down some path that goes nowhere" (Ephesians 4:1 MSG). I love the way *The Message* paraphrase describes his call to action.

Friend, whether you are a walker or runner, today you are called to move forward with purpose, following God. You do not need to walk alone. Let's be known as men and women who walk with God.

FAITH STEP: Have you ever had a walking or running buddy? Is there someone you have stayed in step with in a race or through the years? Reflect on what that experience was like for you. On your next run or walk, imagine pacing with God in the same way. Talk to Him. Walk with Him. Abide in Him.

INSPIRATION: "I ran and ran and ran every day, and I acquired this sense of determination, this sense of spirit that I would never, never give up, no matter what else happened."

　—WILMA RUDOLPH, three-time Olympic champion in the 1960 Rome Olympics (100m, 200m, 400m relay)

NOTES FROM COACH SHAWN: In a marathon, if you are going to walk, walk fast. This will save you considerable time in the race. Pump your arms as if you are running and walk tall without slouching over.

Use the space below to jot down some notes about your daily workouts or goals.

SUNDAY   MILES

MONDAY   MILES _____

TUESDAY   MILES _____

WEDNESDAY   MILES _____

THURSDAY   MILES _____

FRIDAY   MILES _____

SATURDAY   MILES _____

TOTAL MILES _____

4

HE REFRESHES MY SOUL

He leads me beside quiet waters, he refreshes my soul. He
guides me along the right paths for his name's sake.

Psalm 23:2–3

FAITH FUEL

I messaged a few of my mama-runner friends on Friday night to
see if they'd like to go for a trail run. We rose before the sun and
packed into two cars with our snacks and gear. The undulating
green hills and the music of water lapping at the shore beckoned
me. We drove about twenty minutes to the Winchell Cove Trail
at Millerton Lake. This trail is a place of respite—a home away
from home for me.

I started running trails with my mama friends a few months
after my first husband's death. I ran track in high school and dozens of road races prior to that, but there was something about the
trail that was different. It's challenging, but I just can't get enough

of the wildflowers chasing around each curve in the spring or the rainbow sherbet colors of the sunrise dancing over the mountains.

We call ourselves the Go Mama Runners. We are a motley crew of women who walk/run/jog at different paces. A few years ago, we made running tank tops that pretty much sum up what we are about. The back of the tanks say: "Escaping the chaos. Enjoying the trails. Embracing the community."

On the trails, I've learned to take off my competitive hat and simply enjoy the journey. I don't worry about my pace or passing the next person. I simply look for glimpses of God's glory and run. As it says in Psalm 23, He leads me beside quiet waters and refreshes my soul. I find myself in a posture of worship as my trail shoes burrow through the dirt.

Studies show that just ten minutes of walking in nature can help boost your mood, reduce stress and anxiety, and help with schoolwork. I've certainly found this to be true. When I'm out on the trail, God ministers to my soul, and my mood shifts. There are times when my heart is heavy with grief or worry. If I carve out time for a trail run, I begin to work out those feelings. I drink in the sounds and sights of His creation. I feel His comfort in the sway of tree branches and the symphony of birds.

In Psalm 23, David talks about how the Lord is his shepherd, his guide. When we follow Him down life's trail, our souls are refreshed, restored, and renewed. Running or walking then becomes a kind of self-care—or more accurately, soul care. He shows us the path both physically and emotionally so we can step forward.

On that particular Saturday at Winchell Cove, I explored a new part of the trail. I ran with a spirit of wonder and anticipation, looking always for that next right step as the path took me up a steep hill, around a curve looking out at the glassy lake, and then back through dew-heavy grasses. I have learned that sometimes the path before us is unexpected, but God assures me when I'm running that He is leading.

FAITH STEP: Do you live near a trail or a path where you can see God's creation? Take some time for a trail walk or run this week and jot down or snap a few pictures of beautiful things you see along the way. What sights, sounds, smells, or textures help calm your soul?

INSPIRATION: "Finish every workout exhilarated, not exhausted."

—BILL BOWERMAN, legendary track-and-field coach for the University of Oregon (1948–1972) and co-founder of Nike

NOTES FROM COACH SHAWN: Vary your workouts to keep things interesting and fresh. Try running on hills, on flats, on roads, on trails, or possibly run your favorite loop in the opposite direction.

Use the space below to jot down some notes about your daily workouts or goals.

SUNDAY   MILES

MONDAY   MILES

TUESDAY   MILES

WEDNESDAY   MILES

THURSDAY   MILES

FRIDAY   MILES _____

SATURDAY   MILES _____

                                    TOTAL MILES _____

5

YOUR PACE IS YOUR PACE

For we are his workmanship, created in Christ Jesus for good works, which God prepared beforehand, that we should walk in them.

Ephesians 2:10 ESV

FAITH FUEL

The Hensley Lake Off Road race is a 10K that chases along a single track over the undulating hills near Hensley Lake. I've run on this trail several times with friends, but it's always different to run an actual race on a trail.

On race day, we took off at the sound of the bullhorn. Since the trail is narrow, runners quickly have to fall into a single-file line for the first mile of this race. It's hard to pass or run a different pace once you get into that line, which can be frustrating for some runners. Later in the race, the path widens, and runners can spread out more.

When I started out, I recalled the words of one of my writer-mentor friends, Emily P. Freeman: "Your pace is your pace." That little motto applies to running, writing, and life. It's so easy to get caught up in comparisons. We see our friend running faster than us, or that guy who works next to us in the office who got a promotion, or that mama of five from church who seems to be a parenting pro, and then we start to measure ourselves against that person.

Don't get me wrong, I'm competitive. I've seen athletes excel when they have someone to chase, someone to push them to work harder and run faster. But there's a difference between a competitiveness that helps us do our best and comparison that leads to jealousy, envy, and bitterness toward another person.

Whenever I find myself getting discouraged or focused on comparison, I cling to the words of Ephesians 2:10 that remind me I am God's workmanship. "For we are his workmanship, created in Christ Jesus for good works, which God prepared beforehand, that we should walk in them" (Ephesians 2:10 ESV). Some versions use the word *handiwork* or *masterpiece*. We are uniquely created by God to walk, run, and soar on specific paths that He lays out for each one of us. If we are so focused on comparing ourselves to others on the trail, we might miss the specific path God has marked out for us.

The Hensley Lake Off Road race concludes with three steep hills. I heard cheering as I approached the bottom of the final hill. Many of the spectators had hiked to the top of that hill to cheer on their people. Their enthusiasm gave me that extra push to start swinging my arms and climb step by step. My calves burned. My breathing grew heavy. Then I heard my daughters and husband cheering for me. I crested the hill and finished the race. I ran at my personal best pace, and that made all the difference.

Friend, be kind to yourself as you run today. Trust your training. Let your pace be your pace. Give yourself grace on the trail if you aren't as far or as fast as you'd like. You were uniquely created and prepared for this.

FAITH STEP: How can you pivot away from comparison? Write down one lie you have been allowing yourself to listen to lately. Now cross it out and replace it with the truth you know from God's Word. Read the words of Ephesians 2:10 every time you go out for a run this week.

INSPIRATION: "Victory is in having done your best. If you've done your best, you've won."

—BILL BOWERMAN, legendary track-and-field coach for the University of Oregon (1948–1972) and co-founder of Nike.

NOTES FROM COACH SHAWN: Regardless what level of runner you are, be grateful that you can run. Focus on improving your own pace and setting your own personal records rather than comparing yourself to others. Everyone has different life challenges; we are not all beginning from the same starting line.

Use the space below to jot down some notes about your daily workouts or goals.

SUNDAY   MILES _____

MONDAY   MILES _____

TUESDAY   MILES _____

WEDNESDAY   MILES _____

THURSDAY	MILES

FRIDAY	MILES

SATURDAY	MILES

TOTAL MILES _____

6

CLOUD OF WITNESSES

Therefore, since we are surrounded by such a great cloud of witnesses, let us throw off everything that hinders and the sin that so easily entangles. And let us run with perseverance the race marked out for us, fixing our eyes on Jesus, the pioneer and perfecter of faith.

Hebrews 12:1–2

FAITH FUEL

My husband, Shawn, and I began to inch toward the start line. Throngs of runners from a hundred countries around the world joined us for this epic race—the 40th Chicago Marathon. I tried not to focus on my nervousness and instead enjoy the experience of being there with so many people chasing the finish line.

About a year before, I started dreaming up ways to celebrate my fortieth birthday. Running the Chicago Marathon in my home city seemed like the perfect goal to work toward with Shawn as my new running partner and coach. Training for the marathon was a gift mixed with grief. My first husband, Ericlee, soared to heaven in his fortieth year of life.

As the announcer signaled the start, I felt a surge of excitement. We began to navigate the streets and neighborhoods of Chicago. I tackled one mile at a time instead of ruminating on the entire 26.2 miles before me.

With 44,000 runners, I had to do a lot of weaving to find a path for my feet. You don't want to cut anyone off, but you also don't want to get stuck behind a group running a slower pace. Runners elbowed and pushed me more than once. My hubby-coach ran next to me, stride for stride. I steadied the cadence of my breathing.

The words of Hebrews 12:1–3, which I was memorizing at the time, provided inspiration for the race ahead. At mile three we passed our "great cloud of witnesses," including my parents, three daughters, my sister's and brother's families, and some friends who have become like family through the years. They motivated us with smiles, high fives, hugs, and hand-decorated signs. Not only were we surrounded by more than 1.5 million fans lining the streets of Chicago, but we were accompanied by *our* people.

I reflected on how critical the support of my people has been through the years. My tribe has cheered me on at races, the births of my girls, graduations, weddings, and other life events, both difficult and glorious. Maybe you have people who have showed up and consistently cheered you on. Their encouragement buoys our strength.

As I ran the race, I could almost hear my first husband cheering from heaven. I imagined him pumping his fist and calling out in his bellowing coaching voice. I thought of the others gathering in heaven to witness my race—people like my grandparents on both sides, many dear friends, and other heroes of the faith. This is the power of community.

People say that 80 percent of running a marathon is the mental game. My mind started to spiral downward after mile fifteen. The temperature was rising. With each plodding step, I knew I had to rally.

I whispered the words, "*And let us run with perseverance the race marked out for us . . .* " That word *perseverance* lingered in my mind. Perseverance means "to persist in spite of difficulty, obstacles, or discouragement." I have learned on my journey that the best way to navigate grief, to tackle impossible assignments, to face tough conversations is to lean in, to take the next step, and the next. Before I knew it, we were at mile twenty.

At mile twenty-two, a woman cheered us on with surprising passion. Her powerful words were like a victory speech that spoke truth and life into me. She reminded me that the marathon is about grit and glory. Each of us has to run the race marked out just for us.

I'm not going to lie. Those last 4.2 miles were not easy. I could feel the chafing beneath my shirt. I kept drinking water but remained thirsty. Everyone around me was walking. I was tempted to stop, but I couldn't. Shawn started running just ahead of me. He was pacing me. He knew I needed someone to chase. I fixed my eyes on his neon yellow "Run Big" shirt.

The words "*fixing our eyes on Jesus, the pioneer and perfecter of faith*" were cycling through my mind. Sometimes our race is not what we hoped for or expected. It's easy to focus our eyes on our shortcomings and disappointments. Hebrews 12 reminds us where to fix our eyes—on Jesus. He's the pioneer, the first, the one blazing the trail, my pacer for life.

We had one last hill to climb and then we turned the corner. That bright red banner screaming FINISH was my invitation. I shifted to that last gear and ran my guts out. All for His glory!

FAITH STEP: Who are some of the people who are cheering you on in the race of life? How do they encourage you to persevere? Take a moment today to thank them for being your "cloud of witnesses."

INSPIRATION: "Separate your identity from what you do. . . . Understand that running is something that you are really good at. It's a passion. Embrace how much you care about the sport. But always remember it isn't who you are."

—Professional running coach STEVE MAGNESS

NOTES FROM COACH SHAWN: On your birthday, try running a birthday set. Incorporate your age into a workout that will stretch your limits. (Warning: Be sure you have trained properly for it!) For example, run as many miles (or kilometers) as your age, run as many 200-meter intervals as your age, or possibly as many minutes as your age. This is a fun way to celebrate your birthday.

Use the space below to jot down some notes about your daily workouts or goals.

SUNDAY	MILES _____

MONDAY	MILES _____

TUESDAY	MILES _____

WEDNESDAY	MILES _____

THURSDAY	MILES _____

FRIDAY	MILES _____

SATURDAY	MILES _____

TOTAL MILES _____

7

HYDRATING WELL

Jesus said to her, "Everyone who drinks of this water will be thirsty again, but whoever drinks of the water that I will give him will never be thirsty again. The water that I will give him will become in him a spring of water welling up to eternal life."

John 4:13–14 ESV

FAITH FUEL

I started running in grade school. My friend Alia and I would always race the boys at recess with our big '80s hair flowing behind us. Alia's legs were a little longer than mine, and she was just a little faster. I loved to chase her, and we frequently beat the boys in our class.

As I grew older, I started running local 5Ks and 10Ks with my dad. In high school, I made a deal with the soccer/track coach that I would join the track team if he let me play on the boys' soccer team. (Our small private school didn't have a girls' team.) Once I joined the track team, I was hooked. There was nothing like the exhilaration I felt coming from behind in a race and sprinting across that finish line.

Today, I coach my daughters' cross-country and track-and-field teams with Shawn. We constantly coach our athletes about the importance of not just training well, but hydrating well. You can't quickly drink water before a race and think that's going to cut it. I've learned the hard way what it feels like to run a long race with "cotton mouth." Thirst can't be quenched at that point. You have to faithfully drink water for days *before* a big race to prepare your body.

Our bodies are made up of cells that are mostly composed of water. When we drink water, we replenish those cells and keep the blood flowing. We compete best when blood and oxygen are moving freely through our bodies. When we hydrate well, it also allows us to sweat, which keeps the body from overheating.

The same principle of hydration is true in our spiritual lives. As Christians, we can't expect quick sips at the drinking fountain to suffice, especially when we're faced with a daunting emotional, physical, or relationship task. We need to drink deeply of the living water so we have energy and resources for running our daily races.

Jesus unfolded this concept of Living Water in John 4 when He talked to the Samaritan woman at the well. Most Jewish men would have avoided talking to a Samaritan woman, but Jesus spoke directly to her because He had something important to offer. Jesus always moved outside cultural expectations to connect with people's hearts.

Jesus saw her need and offered her living water, which far surpassed anything she could draw from a well. The *water*—Jesus himself—satisfied her thirst for real love. She'd walked to the well, burdened by guilt, shame, and emptiness. She was parched. But after hearing from Jesus, her heart was soaring. She rushed—she RAN—to tell others about her encounter with the Messiah.

Too often we settle for quick sips at the drinking fountain instead of actually taking time to hydrate well and prepare for the next leg of life's race. When we are parched spiritually, we worry more and feel stressed out. Ask God to help you release your worries and anxiety for today and find more space so you can drink from His living water.

You can hydrate well in many practical ways: reading your Bible at a certain time each day; praying while you run; choosing to listen to worship music filled with God's truth instead of music that offers empty, dust-dry entertainment. Consistently seek to connect with God in ways that replenish your soul to keep hydrated for whatever lies ahead.

FAITH STEP: Fill a water bottle and carry it with you so you can hydrate throughout the day. As you drink, memorize these words from Jesus in John 10:10: "I came that they may have life and have it abundantly" (ESV).

INSPIRATION: "Training is not only what you do in official workouts. Training is also how you work, how you eat, how you rest. In other words, how you live."

—RENATO CANOVA, famed coach of many of the top distance runners in the world

NOTES FROM COACH SHAWN: During a run, if your heart rate seems high for your effort level and pace, it may be a sign that you are dehydrated. After a run, be sure to replace all the fluids you lost during running. An effective method to determine how much liquid you sweated out on a run is to weigh yourself before and after a run. Continue to drink enough fluids until your urine is light yellow.

Use the space below to jot down some notes about your daily workouts or goals.

SUNDAY   MILES _____

MONDAY   MILES _____

TUESDAY   MILES _____

WEDNESDAY   MILES _____

THURSDAY   MILES _____

FRIDAY   MILES _____

SATURDAY   MILES _____

TOTAL MILES _____

8

RUNNING AWAY FROM THE LIES

We demolish arguments and every pretension that sets itself up against the knowledge of God, and we take captive every thought to make it obedient to Christ.

2 Corinthians 10:5

FAITH FUEL

That morning I woke to the sound of raindrops tap-dancing on the roof. I begged Shawn to let us skip our run and stay home in bed. He knows me well. He knows I would have regretted it later had I not gotten out there. Without saying a word, my hubby-coach patiently waited for me by the door until I was ready.

We started out slowly in the dark with raindrops splashing in our faces. I was tempted to complain and feel sorry for myself as goose bumps formed on my cold skin. Instead, we distracted ourselves with a new setting I found on my Runkeeper app that allows me to change the voice prompts. Instead of listening to the usual Runner Lady voice relating my pace and timing, I chose Boston Fan.

Shawn and I couldn't stop giggling at Boston Fan's accent. We kept waiting for what he would say next. He kept us going with funny lines like: "Your haht is beating wicked fast, kid," "Greeeeeat job," and "How 'bout them apples?" or "You're ready for the marathon, kid."

How different life would be if we tuned in to the voice of our Biggest Fan instead of our inner Runner Lady/Guy who tells us we are too old, too slow, too heavy, too broken and bruised, too scarred for this life race.

What if, instead, we listened for God's voice like the Boston Fan cheering us on? We so often listen to the lies in our head instead of claiming the truth the Bible tells us. I'm a visual person. I imagine these lies scrawled on the wallpaper of my mind. Any time I find myself lingering over those lies, I go over to the wall and rip that paper down. Then I start putting up new wallpaper covered with truth and beauty.

Friend, when you hear, "You can never escape your past failures," remember, "If anyone is in Christ, he is a new creation. The old has passed away; behold, the new has come" (2 Corinthians 5:17 ESV).

When you hear, "People are going to judge you," remember, "No weapon that is fashioned against you shall succeed, and you shall refute every tongue that rises against you in judgment" (Isaiah 54:17 ESV).

When you hear, "You are not good enough, fast enough, strong enough," answer with this: "But he said to me, 'My grace is sufficient for you, for my power is made perfect in weakness.' Therefore I will boast all the more gladly about my weaknesses, so that Christ's power may rest on me" (2 Corinthians 12:9 ESV).

Each one of us is part of God's glory story. Let's run away from the lies and into the truth we know from God. Paul reminds us in 2 Corinthians 10:5 to "take captive every thought to make it obedient to Christ." Let's chase His glory together as we sprint for the day's finish line.

FAITH STEP: What are some of the lies you've been telling yourself lately? Write them down. Then take time to write out today's Living Water Scripture or another Scripture that reminds you of who you are in Christ. Pray for God to help you run away from the lies and toward the truth.

INSPIRATION: "It's very hard in the beginning to understand that the whole idea is not to beat the other runners. Eventually you learn that the competition is against the little voice inside you that wants you to quit."

   —DR. GEORGE A. SHEEHAN, author of several running books

NOTES FROM COACH SHAWN: Eat a well-balanced diet of carbohydrates, protein, and fat for optimal performance. Although complex carbohydrates are a favorite for distance runners for energy, protein is also necessary for regenerating broken-down muscles. Stay clear of unsustainable fad diets and quick weight-loss methods.

Use the space below to jot down some notes about your daily workouts or goals.

SUNDAY   MILES _____

MONDAY   MILES _____

TUESDAY   MILES _____

WEDNESDAY   MILES _____

THURSDAY   MILES _____

FRIDAY   MILES _____

SATURDAY   MILES _____

TOTAL MILES _____

9

SEASONED WITH SALT

"You are the salt of the earth. But what good is salt if it has lost its flavor? Can you make it salty again? It will be thrown out and trampled underfoot as worthless."

Matthew 5:13 NLT

FAITH FUEL

Your face is painted with salty lines. Your lips and arms sport a crusty, white residue. This could be a sign that your body needs to rehydrate and replenish its salt. Maybe you've had the following experience after running a marathon or a 10K.

Salt—sodium chloride—helps our cells function, enables our nerves to transmit impulses, and stimulates muscle fibers. The recommended daily allowance is 2,300 milligrams, but we can sweat out as much as 3,000 milligrams in an hour of hard training. We need salt to help regulate our bodies. The more I've trained and run in longer races, the more I've learned how vital salt is to my running and recovery. I used to struggle with severe headaches after long runs. My husband suggested I take a salt tablet before and/or partway through my long runs. (You can buy a bottle of ingestible salt tablets online or at most running stores.) This has been a game changer for me. I've also learned that a salty snack like potato chips or a bowl of chicken noodle soup after a long run helps with quick recovery.

Throughout most of history, salt has been a prized commodity. Salt adds flavor and can be used as a preservative. In limited amounts, salt suppresses bitterness and enhances sweetness.

Recently, I was teaching a cooking class at my kids' school. We were making pizza dough. The recipe called for less than a quarter of a teaspoon of salt, but the kids understood that even a small amount of salt could make a big difference in the batch of dough.

In the Sermon on the Mount, Jesus talks about how as believers we are to be salt and light in the world. Jesus says, "You are the salt of the earth. But what good is salt if it has lost its flavor? Can you make it salty again? It will be thrown out and trampled underfoot as worthless" (Matthew 5:13 NLT).

We are called to preserve and add flavor to the world like salt. Jesus also refers to the important influence the disciples had on the body of believers. By encouraging and teaching, the disciples could help preserve their faith. Friend, how can you add flavor and bring value to your family and community? How can you invest in your relationship with Jesus Christ and preserve a godly lifestyle? How can you be salt and light to the world around you?

I don't want to have an unregulated body because of lack of salt. And I don't want my life to resemble tasteless salt that has no influence or impact on others. I long to be like the salt Jesus talks about—salt that flavors, preserves, and brings out the best in others.

FAITH STEP: From your cabinet, take out whatever salt you have on hand. Sprinkle a few grains into your palm. Taste the salt as you pray about areas where you can be salt and light to the people around you. Write down one way you hope to preserve the flavor of your faith this week.

INSPIRATION: "Most runners run not because they want to live longer, but because they want to live life to the fullest."

—HARUKI MURAKAMI, Japanese writer

NOTES FROM COACH SHAWN: If you are running long in hot weather, it may be helpful to eat salty foods and/or add salt to your food a day or two prior to the run. Salt helps your body retain water that your muscles need to function. When you are sweating heavily during a run, you will lose a lot of salt. It needs to be replaced. Taking salt tablets during a run may also help reduce muscle cramps.

Use the space below to jot down some notes about your daily workouts or goals.

SUNDAY	MILES

MONDAY	MILES

TUESDAY	MILES

WEDNESDAY	MILES

THURSDAY   MILES _____

FRIDAY   MILES _____

SATURDAY   MILES _____

                                     TOTAL MILES _____

10

RUNNING THROUGH LIFE'S HURDLES

Consider it pure joy, my brothers and sisters, whenever you face trials of many kinds, because you know that the testing of your faith produces perseverance. Let perseverance finish its work so that you may be mature and complete, not lacking anything.

James 1:2–4

FAITH FUEL

Coach Churchill mostly had me run middle-distance races until this one particular track meet. Coach walked up to me and said, "Hey, how would you like to run hurdles today?"

I raised an eyebrow at him. Coach Churchill, whom we fondly called "Church," had a way of pushing me and challenging me to attempt new things. "I've never run hurdles before," I responded.

"I know," Church said. "I'll teach you."

That was the day I fell in love with the 300-meter hurdles. Church gave me a quick lesson. I practiced a few times, and then I went to the starting line. There wasn't time to get too nervous. There were only a handful of girls in the race that day.

I'm sure I didn't have great form or strategy in that race, but I immediately fell in love with the challenge. I loved the feeling of soaring over those hurdles and the thrill of coming from behind to win the race.

After that, I worked with another teacher who ran hurdles in college. Mr. Kritzberg taught me that I had to learn to run *through* the hurdles, not over them. In other words, he didn't want me to jump over them. He wanted me to keep a steady cadence and lift my legs slightly to get over them. Then I was supposed to snap my lead leg back down and keep running.

If I spent too much time focusing on the hurdle itself or worrying about falling, then I would sacrifice my speed. The goal was to simply graze over the hurdles and keep my eyes on the finish line.

Hurdles are like the obstacles and challenges we face in our life. In James 1:2, we are encouraged to consider it joy when we face trials in our lives because this produces perseverance. Sometimes it's hard to approach life's hurdles with joy. Maybe you've recently lost your job or you're navigating tension in your marriage. Maybe you've been traversing infertility or battling depression. These are big life hurdles.

When we see hurdles in the lane in front us, we can get caught up in thinking about the worst-case scenarios and the hardships to come. We can start to obsess about how the race will turn out instead of taking that courageous step forward.

Even if you're not physically running over hurdles this week, there are hurdles we all must face in our training, our races, and our lives. Friend, don't focus on the obstacle. Keep your eyes on the horizon and run through. Let perseverance finish its work and carry you to the finish line.

FAITH STEP: Jot down a list of some of the hurdles in your life right now. Visualize yourself running through those hurdles in a race. Ask God to grow perseverance in you during this season.

INSPIRATION: "It wasn't easy, but I tried my best and I was able to do so many things that I would have not done had I just given up on my life when it was hard. So I guess my message is that it's okay to struggle but it's not okay to give up on yourself or your dreams."

— GABE GRUNEWALD, 2014 USA indoor track-and-field 3,000m champion; battled cancer from 2009–2019

NOTES FROM COACH SHAWN: Regularly take a couple of minutes to visualize yourself racing. Play over in your mind how you will respond to fatigue, opponents, and unexpected obstacles along the course.

Use the space below to jot down some notes about your daily workouts or goals.

SUNDAY	MILES

MONDAY	MILES

TUESDAY	MILES

WEDNESDAY	MILES

THURSDAY   MILES _____

FRIDAY   MILES _____

SATURDAY   MILES _____

TOTAL MILES _____

11

PRESS ON TOWARD
THE GOAL

Brothers [and sisters], I do not consider that I have made it
my own. But one thing I do: forgetting what lies behind and
straining forward to what lies ahead, I press on toward the goal
for the prize of the upward call of God in Christ Jesus.

Philippians 3:13–14 ESV

FAITH FUEL

For years we have hosted a family track night on Thursdays at
the local high school track. This is a highlight for the members of
our Remember Haiti Half Marathon training team. The mamas
bring cooler bags filled with fruit strips, Popsicles, cheese sticks,
and drinks. We spread picnic blankets and let the kids run free
in the grass in the middle of the track that doubles as a football
field. The older kids keep watch of the little ones while parents
walk, jog, and sprint around the track. In recent years, some of
the grade-school kids have joined us in training.

Workouts on the track always energize me, especially when the temperature cools even a few degrees on a late August evening. Even though we all jog or run at different paces, we can more easily cheer each other on at the track because we pass each other more often. And we usually start with a whole-team warm-up—a combination of dynamic exercises and stretches that help us get ready for the workout.

My hubby-coach, Shawn, explains that track workouts are an opportunity for runners to learn how to pace themselves, how to run at faster speeds, and how to improve their running form. He builds interval workouts for our team. Sometimes we run 400s (one full loop around the track) with rests in between. Other times we'll tackle a workout with varying distances and speeds.

Maybe it's because I was a track athlete in my younger days that I always feel freer to go all-out on the track. The boundaries and lanes are clearly drawn. The finish line is always in sight. My body and muscles remember the distances. I know at the final 50 meters it's time to just sprint my heart out to the finish.

In Philippians 3, the apostle Paul is writing from prison in Rome while awaiting his sentence. Paul must have been a runner or a huge fan of the original Olympic games, because he uses the metaphor of running several times throughout his letters.

In Philippians 3:13–14, he urges the believers in the city of Philippi to persevere with purpose to the finish line. He writes, "But one thing I do: forgetting what lies behind and straining forward to what lies ahead, I press on toward the goal for the prize of the upward call of God in Christ Jesus." In this context, we can assume that Paul most looked forward to being *with Christ* in eternity. And he was encouraging his fellow believers to press on toward the same goal and prize as well.

Just as Paul urges the Philippians to lift their eyes from their own suffering to see the joy ahead, we also must challenge ourselves to rejoice through the trials and run all-out for the finish line in our lives.

On the track, we watch the sun get lower and lower with each lap we run. We press on toward the finish before darkness sets in. On my final lap, I strain forward and cross the line just in time to see the colors of the sunset stacked in layers like a rainbow-frosted cake. Candy-apple red meets deep amethyst meets ripe peach. This view is my prize tonight, standing witness to the hard work of training on the track and my Jesus, who meets me at the finish line.

FAITH STEP: What is one thing or attitude that is holding you back in this season of life? Imagine yourself letting that thing go and running all-out for the finish line. At the end of your next run, practice sprinting for the last twenty seconds or 50 meters.

INSPIRATION: "I simply try to do this through my results, and compare my career to climbing a tree. I'm always trying to climb up to the next branch and forget what I've left behind."

—GEOFFREY KAMWOROR, 2017 New York City Marathon champion

NOTES FROM COACH SHAWN: At the end of long runs, gradually increase your pace the last mile and envision yourself during the last mile of your upcoming goal event. This will give you practice for finishing strong on race day.

Use the space below to jot down some notes about your daily workouts or goals.

SUNDAY   MILES

MONDAY   MILES

| TUESDAY | MILES _____ |

| WEDNESDAY | MILES _____ |

| THURSDAY | MILES _____ |

| FRIDAY | MILES _____ |

| SATURDAY | MILES _____ |

TOTAL MILES _____

12

TRUST YOUR COACH

Trust in the Lord with all your heart and lean not on your own understanding.

Proverbs 3:5

FAITH FUEL

This morning Shawn and I ran a familiar trail in Baltimore, Maryland, not far from his old town house. He lived in Baltimore for nine years and considers it a golden season of his single-guy life. We returned this weekend to attend a good friend's wedding.

Shawn led our run on a paved path through the forest and behind neighborhoods. The ground was carpeted with lush grasses and green foliage. The path curved and rolled up and down, at times jogging alongside a creek.

Once again, I found myself marveling at all God has led me through these past five years. I ran this trail with my late husband, Ericlee, in 2008 when we were visiting our friend Shawn, and then again on my own in 2010 when my mom and I visited on our way to Washington, D.C., for a book award. In 2015, I ran this trail again when Shawn and I had just started dating.

On the way back to our hotel, Shawn took an early turn and we were suddenly on a much steeper uphill climb than anticipated. I started to doubt if I should be following this guy, especially when two dogs started fiercely barking at us. But I have learned to trust my husband.

The word *trust* shows up more than 160 times throughout the Bible. This concept of trust is an integral part of the Christian faith. When we trust someone, it means we put our hope and confidence in that person. It means we believe in them and rely on them. God invites us to trust Him on life's trails. He doesn't promise the path will be without hills and curves, but He does say He will guide us.

That turn Shawn took that led us uphill soon revealed itself to be a shortcut that returned us to our original path. I tend to be more of a leader than a follower, but I was reminded that it's a gift to be able to follow someone I trust, who always has my best interest in mind. How much more has my heavenly Father shown me this too!

Proverbs 3:5 reminds us, "Trust in the LORD with all your heart and lean not on your own understanding." Sometimes it's easier said than done. I often long for a preview and understanding of the details.

When I'm having a hard time trusting God, I try to refer back to the times when I've trusted Him in the past and He's proved trustworthy. I think about when I felt called to quit my job as a newspaper reporter and take an opportunity to move to Haiti to teach English. That decision didn't make logical sense when I had worked so hard to get the position at the newspaper, but I profoundly sensed that God was leading me.

That trip to Haiti in 2002 proved to be a turning point in my life. God led me to new passions and new friends, and eventually helped connect me with my late husband, Ericlee, and my now hubby-coach, Shawn.

Looking back, I'm glad God didn't give me all the details in advance. I needed to learn to trust Him, to walk with Him step by step, so eventually I could soar in new ways.

FAITH STEP: Can you think of an area or two where God is calling you to trust Him? If you write in your Bible, consider jotting it down in the margin next to Proverbs 3:5. Let Him guide you and see what unfolds. Thank Him for directing your path.

INSPIRATION: "Man's ambitions don't diminish over time, they grow—and not just the ambitions, but the preparation too."

—GEBRE GEBREMARIAM, 2010 New York City Marathon champion

NOTES FROM COACH SHAWN: Before embarking on any hard interval workouts, run at least three times per week for a month. During that month, include some 30- to 60-second gradual surges during your run at least once a week to prepare your legs and your lungs for higher intensity interval sessions. Also, at the conclusion of each run, perform three to four strides of 75 meters where you focus on running with good form and at a fast but very controlled pace.

Use the space below to jot down some notes about your daily workouts or goals.

SUNDAY   MILES _____

MONDAY   MILES _____

TUESDAY	MILES _____

WEDNESDAY	MILES _____

THURSDAY	MILES _____

FRIDAY	MILES _____

SATURDAY	MILES _____

TOTAL MILES _____

13

GET UP AND WALK

Then Jesus said to him, "Get up! Pick up your mat and walk."
At once the man was cured; he picked up his mat and walked.

John 5:8–9

FAITH FUEL

Sometimes the physical movement of running can provide an opportunity for God to work emotional healing in our lives.

Through the years, I've talked to other friends who have used running, walking, and even hiking as a kind of therapy to get them through life's most difficult trials. My friend Tamara shared about how getting up to run at 4:30 a.m. and chasing the goal to run a marathon helped her through the hardest days of a divorce process. She told herself if she could make it through a run, she could make it through the day.

My widow-friend, Melissa, joined a local hiking group several years after her husband's death. She was pregnant with twins when he died and had to go into survival mode. She described how years later, these hikes gave her physical space to breathe and emotional space to grieve. She eventually hiked Machu Picchu in Peru—a goal she never imagined accomplishing.

Studies show that exercise has not only physical health benefits, but mental and psychological benefits too. Running, walking, and hiking actually affects our brains; God designed exercise as a pathway to healing. In John 5, Jesus goes to Jerusalem to a pool called Bethesda, which means "house of mercy." This pool was one of the deep stone reservoirs that collected rainwater to be used as drinking water. This was a gathering place for the sick and physically disabled. Jesus notices a man there who had been sick for thirty-eight years. He asks him, "Do you want to get well?" (John 5:6).

The man does not recognize Jesus and doesn't understand this key question. The man says he has no one to help him get into the pool where many were healed. It's no accident that Jesus has mercy on him at the "house of mercy."

"Then Jesus said to him, 'Get up! Pick up your mat and walk.' At once the man was cured; he picked up his mat and walked" (John 5:8–9). Jesus proves *himself* as the Healer—not the pool at Bethesda, which people believed had healing properties in itself.

Jesus also gives these three directives: get up, pick up your mat, and walk. In other places in Scripture, Jesus gives similar directives when He heals someone. In Matthew 9:6, Jesus heals a paralyzed man and says, "Get up, take your mat and go home." When He orders both of these men to take up their mats or their beds, it's as if to say, "It's time to move out of this place of sickness and pain and make your home in healing."

In Mark 5:41–42, Jesus raises a girl from the dead. "He took her by the hand and said to her, *'Talitha koum!'* (which means 'Little girl, I say to you, get up!'). Immediately the girl stood up and began to walk around." She too is given a hand by Jesus to "get up and walk" in healing. These examples serve as reminders that Jesus can heal us and guide us into a new life, but we have to trust Him, get up, and walk!

FAITH STEP: Is there something in your life that you need healing for today? Why do you think Jesus asked the sick man that poignant question: "Do you want to get well?" If Jesus asked you that question, how would you respond? Take some time to journal your response.

INSPIRATION: "I made it a point to stop trying to have a victim mentality or to say, 'poor me,' or 'why is this happening?' I was like, all right, you have to get this done. . . . As an athlete, you have to truly believe deep down to your core that you're going to get through this and come back and be just as strong as you were before."

—GALEN RUPP, American distance runner and two-time Olympic medalist, discussing his mentality about needing heel surgery

NOTES FROM COACH SHAWN: When you begin to feel the onset of an injury, immediately reduce your running volume and intensity. It's better to sacrifice a couple of runs upfront rather than risk more serious injury that necessitates resting for weeks or even months.

Use the space below to jot down some notes about your daily workouts or goals.

SUNDAY	MILES

MONDAY	MILES

TUESDAY	MILES

WEDNESDAY   MILES _____

THURSDAY   MILES _____

FRIDAY   MILES _____

SATURDAY   MILES _____

TOTAL MILES _____

14

LEARNING TO BREATHE

"I will make breath enter you, and you will come to life. I will attach tendons to you and make flesh come upon you and cover you with skin; I will put breath in you, and you will come to life. Then you will know that I am the LORD."

Ezekiel 37:5–6

FAITH FUEL

Breathe in deeply. Let the air gently fill your lungs. Pause. Then release. Feel the tension in your shoulders drift away. Inhale again. Then exhale. This is the give and take of breath. This is a deliberate slowing of the cadence of our breath. This is discovering a new, unforced rhythm.

The Hebrew name for God is *Yahweh*. When the Hebrew letters YHWH are pronounced, some have likened it to the sound of taking a deep breath. This connection is no coincidence in my mind, for God himself fashioned Adam from the dust of the earth and breathed life into his lungs.

This past June I took a trip to Colorado and stayed in Estes Park for several days. Estes Park sits at the base of Rocky Mountain National Park at 3,522-feet elevation. One morning I went for a five-mile run on a path not far from our cabin. My chest pulled tight as I tried to fill my lungs. I had to slow down and take shorter breaths. I had to give myself grace that my pace was not as fast as it might be at home, where I live in a valley.

In life, sometimes we find ourselves at an unfamiliar altitude, and we need to take shorter breaths. We need to slow our rhythm to breathe deeply. Maybe you've experienced some trauma in your past or you are presently walking through a crisis, and it feels hard to breathe. These are the times when it is a gift to run alongside others. It's so easy to default into isolation when we feel over-whelmed. When we share our stories, when we bear witness to truth and pain, we offer each other breath. Breathing then comes a little easier. Inhale long. Breathe out.

In Ezekiel 37, the prophet talks about a valley of dry bones—a symbol of lifelessness. God says to these bones, "I will make breath enter you, and you will come to life. I will attach tendons to you and make flesh come upon you and cover you with skin; I will put breath in you, and you will come to life. Then you will know that I am the LORD" (Ezekiel 37:5–6).

Then He breathes into them, and the dry bones miraculously rattle and snap to life. These bones were once dry and dead, but now they are alive and moving. God breathes—sometimes through the stories and encouragement of others—and we come to life.

One of my favorite songs is "Great Are You Lord" by All Sons & Daughters. This song became especially meaningful to me in 2014 when my beloved husband was battling cancer. A couple of friends from the worship band at our church visited our home to sing with my husband.

As they sang and played guitar, my husband sat on our big red couch and listened with a look of contentment on his face.

Our three daughters danced as these worshipful words filled our home. We sang together about how it's His breath in our lungs that causes us to overflow with praise.

Ironically, during that time, the cancer was spreading to my husband's lungs. His breathing was labored. Little did we know that soon he would soar to meet the One who first breathed life into him.

Now I reach for gratitude even when breathing feels hard, like on my run in Colorado. I thank God for my lungs, for this daily cadence of borrowed breaths, and for the privilege of living one more day to reflect His glory.

FAITH STEP: Have you ever run or walked at a higher altitude? What do you remember about that experience? Take some time today to pay attention to your breathing. Before your next run or jog, breathe in slowly through your nose for four counts, and then breathe out through your mouth for four counts. Repeat this eight times.

INSPIRATION: "A race is a work of art that people can look at and be affected in as many ways as they're capable of understanding."

—STEVE PREFONTAINE, American Olympic distance runner during the 1970s

NOTES FROM COACH SHAWN: Until your body adapts to running at high altitudes, ease into a run and slow your pace. If you start running too quickly, your heart rate will spike and it will be challenging to get your breathing under control unless you stop. Also, drink water more liberally throughout a long run since the air is drier.

Use the space below to jot down some notes about your daily workouts or goals.

SUNDAY   MILES _____

MONDAY   MILES _____

TUESDAY   MILES _____

WEDNESDAY   MILES _____

THURSDAY   MILES _____

FRIDAY   MILES _____

SATURDAY   MILES _____

TOTAL MILES _____

15

LOOKING BEYOND
THE HAZE

Everything was created through him; nothing—not one thing!—
came into being without him. What came into existence was Life,
and the Life was Light to live by. The Life-Light blazed out of the
darkness; the darkness couldn't put it out.

John 1:3–5 MSG

FAITH FUEL

As I write this, the temperatures have been soaring above the
hundreds in central California. Yesterday was 106°F. The sky was
gray and hazy. The air was heavy. These triple-digit temperatures
force me into a new rhythm of running much earlier in the day.
Although I'm not a morning person by nature, I'm driven to rise
early to beat the heat.

This morning I ran with my friend Stephanie up the Clovis Trail
near my house. Just as we got past a dark corridor of trees, we saw
the most brilliant sunrise emerging. The sky was a palette of warm

colors—ruby, fuchsia, tangerine, and violet swirling together— against the backdrop of the hazy sky. Throughout our run, we watched as the glowing-orange sun ball climbed higher and higher up the rungs of the sky. It was breathtaking.

This morning's sunrise got me thinking about the wondrous ways God reveals His presence to us when we are facing the heat. When life feels hazy and full of struggle, when the air and atmosphere around us feels heavy, when we are traveling through a dark season, God can show up in unexpected ways with His light.

Like a love letter painted across the sky, He gives you and me glimpses of His glory through a sunrise. He gifts us with joy in the unexpected giggles of a child. Sometimes He redeems a day with an encouraging word, a gift from a friend, or the pale pink roses blooming in our front yard. All of these are examples of His light piercing the darkness.

The theme of light versus darkness is pervasive throughout the Bible. The word *light* is used more than seventy times in the New Testament alone. It's natural for us to be drawn to the light in the same way my friend and I could not keep our eyes off the rising sun.

John introduces his gospel by establishing who Jesus Christ is—the Word, the Creator, the Light. "Everything was created through him; nothing—not one thing!—came into being without him. What came into existence was Life, and the Life was Light to live by. The Life-Light blazed out of the darkness; the darkness couldn't put it out" (John 1:3–5 MSG). This passage underscores how the light overcomes the darkness.

These words are echoed in John 8:12 when Jesus says, "I am the light of the world. Whoever follows me will never walk in darkness, but will have the light of life." Jesus' message in this passage is that we must follow Him if we want to experience eternal life, the light of life.

If you light a candle in a dark room or turn on your phone flashlight as you are ascending a dark staircase, you will see the power of even a small amount of light. That light fills a room and illuminates the path. On some very dark mornings, runners may have to wear a headlamp or lighted vest to see where they are going. There is comfort in the light reflecting on the path and knowing what lies just ahead.

Friend, let me encourage you today that even when the sky is hazy, there is light shining through somewhere. Our friend Jesus longs to shine His light into your darkness. Lift your eyes to the sun and see Him there.

FAITH STEP: Next time you go for a walk or run, notice the light. What are you most drawn to about it? Is the sun rising or setting? How would you describe the colors in the sky today? Write out a little prayer thanking God for the light and what He revealed to you.

INSPIRATION: "If you have a dream, pursue it as hard as you can. The world needs more of that."

—JORDAN RAPP, professional triathlete

NOTES FROM COACH SHAWN: Especially during hot summer days, hydrate properly while running by taking sips of water at least every mile. It may be helpful to carry a water bottle with you (either in your hand or in a waist pack), strategically plant water bottles along your run course before your run, or take a path that has water fountains along the way.

Use the space below to jot down some notes about your daily workouts or goals.

SUNDAY   MILES

MONDAY   MILES _____

TUESDAY   MILES _____

WEDNESDAY   MILES _____

THURSDAY   MILES _____

FRIDAY   MILES _____

SATURDAY   MILES _____

                                    TOTAL MILES _____

16

PERFECT PRACTICE
MAKES PERFECT

Finally, brothers, whatever is true, whatever is honorable, whatever is just, whatever is pure, whatever is lovely, whatever is commendable, if there is any excellence, if there is anything worthy of praise, think about these things. What you have learned and received and heard and seen in me—practice these things, and the God of peace will be with you.

Philippians 4:8–9 ESV

FAITH FUEL

Shawn and I coach the junior high track-and-field team at our daughters' school. Shawn has a few signature sayings he repeats to the kids during practice. One is, "Practice doesn't make perfect. Perfect practice makes perfect."

The first time he said that, I quizzed him. "What does that mean?" I was just as stumped as the kids. Then he explained that it's not enough just to practice something. In fact, there are a lot of wrong ways to practice technique and form, especially for track-and-field events. The old adage says "Practice makes perfect," but Shawn's version adds an important nuance. We can't be lazy during practice, because then our bad habits will show up on race day. We have to be focused, intentional, and attentive. The emphasis is not on being perfect, but on being conscientious as we practice.

We remind the athletes to swing their arms freely, bending at their elbows in a 90-degree position when they run. When they are doing drills, we encourage them to use their opposite leg and arm for balance and a natural running position. We also urge them not to hunch or bend forward too much. These are small adjustments that can make a big difference for a runner, jumper, or thrower. We ask our athletes to show us their best effort in practice.

When Paul writes to the church of Philippi, he similarly urges them to be intentional and conscientious. In Philippians 4, Paul highlights specific values that are key to the Christian life. He writes that we are to "think about things" that are true, honorable, just, pure, lovely, commendable, excellent, or worthy of praise. These values should guide our thoughts and direct our motives. When life is hard or you are filled with anxious thoughts, it's helpful to have an arsenal of truths that can help redirect you.

Why are these specific values noteworthy? I like to break it down by asking myself these questions and reviewing the truths I know:

What is true? His Word; Jesus is the Word become flesh.

What is honorable? His people, when they act with humility and respect.

What is just? God's heart for the vulnerable, including widows, orphans, immigrants, and the poor.

What is pure? Turning away from temptation, asking God to forgive us of our sins.

What is lovely? His created beauty that calms our spirits and fills us with awe.

What is commendable? When a Christ-follower vulnerably shares her or his story for God's glory.

What is excellent? When someone upholds a high standard and puts forth their best effort in their work, inspiring others.

What is worthy of praise? Our God, who gives us good gifts.

Paul says, "Practice these things, and the God of peace will be with you" (Philippians 4:9 ESV). The practice part is important. We have to practice because these things don't necessarily come naturally to us. Practice means performing an activity repeatedly to improve or maintain proficiency. We have to practice good form in running and in our spiritual lives.

The result of practicing or "dwelling on these things," as some versions of the Bible say, is peace. We receive the gift of peace from God when we are intentional about focusing on these things Paul mentions. This is a peace that passes understanding. This is the peace of His presence.

FAITH STEP: Write out your own answers to the questions mentioned above on a note card: What is true? What is honorable? What is just? What is pure? What is lovely? What is commendable? What is excellent? What is worthy of praise? Tuck this note card in your Bible or in your car or tape it to your mirror. When your thoughts turn negative or you feel anxious, meditate on these things.

INSPIRATION: "They eat, sleep and train, they don't have late nights. They watch what they eat. They sleep early. I just thought if I am going to beat these guys one day I am going to have to change my lifestyle."

—MO FARAH, British Olympic champion distance runner, on living with Kenyan runners for a year

NOTES FROM COACH SHAWN: Consistently perform running drills such as high knees, butt kickers, and skipping to enhance muscle memory, flexibility, and coordination. These will help your form and speed, and decrease the risk of injury. As you perform the drills, focus on correct form and don't rush through them.

Use the space below to jot down some notes about your daily workouts or goals.

SUNDAY   MILES _____

MONDAY   MILES _____

TUESDAY   MILES _____

WEDNESDAY   MILES _____

THURSDAY   MILES _____

FRIDAY   MILES _____

SATURDAY   MILES _____

                                            TOTAL MILES _____

17

THE POWER OF SUGGESTION

Therefore encourage one another and build each other up, just as in fact you are doing.

1 Thessalonians 5:11

FAITH FUEL

"You're so good at hills!" A voice bellowed through the corridor of trees and rocks along the San Joaquin River Gorge. I was a little startled at first when I heard the voice behind me. Was he talking to me? I was running the final mile of the San Joaquin River Trail 10K race. There's a pretty hefty uphill before the trail plateaus right at the finish.

In that moment, I was so focused on placing my feet just right on the rocky terrain that I didn't know anyone else was paying attention. Out of the corner of my eye, I saw a guy wearing a bright orange shirt—a stark contrast to the neutral earth tones on the trail. Then he yelled again. "You! Yeah, you! You're so good at hills!"

I turned my head and smiled. I have never thought of myself as particularly strong at running hills, but when this complete stranger called it out, I started to believe it. I got into "the zone" and started hauling up the hill. This was the power of suggestion. He had somehow given me courage to go faster and push harder.

Apparently, suggestion is truly a powerful thing. Research shows that deliberate suggestion can influence how well people remember things, how they respond to medical treatments, and even how well they will perform and behave. Even if someone merely suggests something, it can often cause a person to work harder and bring into reality that thing that was suggested.

Suggestion played a powerful role in my race. My new friend in the orange shirt gave me just the encouragement I needed to get after it. His words reminded me that the last mile is typically my favorite in any distance race because I can just go all-out. There's no need to conserve energy. I run as fast as my legs can take me to the finish line.

The apostle Paul wrote two letters to the church at Thessalonica, which are included in the New Testament. The city of Thessalonica was located on the eastern coast of Macedonia—a strategic location for the advance of the gospel throughout the Roman Empire. Paul wrote to encourage the church to press on, despite the persecution they faced. He urged them to fight up that proverbial hill and run for God's glory. He also instructed them to edify each other on the journey.

Paul writes, "Therefore encourage one another and build each other up, just as in fact you are doing" (1 Thessalonians 5:11). It's important to Paul that the Thessalonians encourage each other in the faith and knowledge that Jesus Christ died for them and would return one day.

Later in my run, I saw the guy in the orange shirt at the finish line. He came up to me and said it again. "You are so good at hills. You blew by me on the trail."

I thanked him for his words of encouragement. I knew in my heart that the power of suggestion is what really helped me soar to the finish.

FAITH STEP: Pray about someone you could encourage this week. Maybe it's a mom, a friend, a mentor, a fellow runner, or a spouse who needs the power of suggestion. Help lift them up by affirming their gifts or encouraging them to pursue a goal. Write a card, send a text, invite them to coffee, or call them on the phone.

INSPIRATION: "Growing up, I wanted to go to the Olympics. I wanted to set world records and set American records. So those things have always been in the back of my mind. . . . I believe that I'm capable of doing that. And that's half the battle, just believing in yourself."

　　—SHELBY HOULIHAN, American women's 5,000m record holder
　　as of July 21, 2018

NOTES FROM COACH SHAWN: Hills are our friends because they make us stronger and improve our running. Running hill intervals increases strength and power, which translates into speed. That's why I call it speed training in disguise. Hills also improve our aerobic fitness by increasing and sustaining our heart rate higher than usual and make running on flat ground feel easy by comparison.

Use the space below to jot down some notes about your daily workouts or goals.

SUNDAY   MILES

MONDAY   MILES _____

TUESDAY   MILES _____

WEDNESDAY   MILES _____

THURSDAY   MILES _____

FRIDAY   MILES _____

SATURDAY   MILES _____

TOTAL MILES _____

18

TRAVERSING LIFE'S TRAILS

Jesus answered, "I am the way and the truth and the life. No one comes to the Father except through me."

John 14:6

FAITH FUEL

A few years ago I ran my first trail race. I'd been a runner all my life, but I had never experienced anything quite like the challenge of that trail run. My friends and I signed up for a 10K. We figured we could do anything for 6.2 miles—even if it meant we had to hike, walk, or crawl. We heard the scenery at the San Joaquin River Gorge Trail (just forty-five minutes from my home in central California) was breathtaking. I longed to try something new.

Let's just say it was hard. While I was running, I kept thinking about how this run mirrored my life. Part of the thrill was that I never knew what to expect. For most distance races, I train, I fuel up, and I settle into a pace after the first mile or two. This was different because I didn't know the path ahead.

In John 14, Jesus is talking to the disciples. He explains that He is going to His Father's house to prepare a place for them. Thomas said to Him, "Lord, we don't know where you are going, so how can we know the way?" (John 14:5).

Jesus answered, "I am the way and the truth and the life. No one comes to the Father except through me" (John 14:6). Jesus is not simply saying He will show them the way; He proclaims that He *is* the way. They will meet His Father through Him. We all gain access to heaven through Him.

On the San Joaquin River Gorge Trail, I couldn't really pace myself. I had to reckon with rocks, slippery dirt, tree roots, blinding sun, bugs, a collection of other runners on the path, and even cows. The first mile of the race turned out to be a surprising downhill. I found myself chatting with my friend Tanya and cruising much faster than my normal pace. I started to believe maybe this race wasn't going to be as hard as I thought.

But downhill can often be deceiving. This is similar to times when our lives are comfortable. On the downhill, we have to be *even more* conscious to stay under control, watch the path for things that might trip us up, and maintain good running form so we don't get hurt along the way.

That first mile downhill was a reminder that I have to be disciplined in the way I actually run the race. Friend, we can't surge ahead of God and run out of control when the path seems easy, because we never know what waits around the bend.

After the first mile, we were guided onto an uphill trail. The path was steep and dusty, twisting and turning. What a contrast to the downhill! I started out feeling strong. I was lifting my knees and pushing through, but after a while I started to grow weary. The path had grown so steep and full of obstacles that I actually had to walk. I felt discouraged and ashamed.

This was much like what I experienced during a hard season of grief. There were many days I felt worn and weary. I was overwhelmed by the steep path ahead. I had to keep walking for the sake of my three young daughters. I had to continue hoping in the Lord.

Walking was not giving up; it was moving forward. And before I knew it, I was over the steepest ridge to a flatter path full of sunshine and green grasses where cows were grazing.

As I continued my run, I leaped over rocks and ducked under tree branches. The pace changed once again. I heard footsteps behind me and someone breathing in my ear. After several minutes of running together, the voice of a woman said, "You are running a great race. Thank you for pacing me."

I laughed. I had no idea where I was going or what pace I was running, but she was depending on me to lead her. My new friend Kimberly was thanking me for running ahead, but she was unknowingly encouraging me on my own journey to keep going. And this is why you and I can't give up running. We don't always know who is gaining courage from following in our footsteps.

After I turned and headed down the path along the river, I started to feel the fatigue set in. I wondered how much longer I had until the finish. I questioned if my legs could keep going. We turned a corner through tall grasses and there it was—the arch with the word FINISH stamped across it.

I broke into a sprint—my last surge of energy. Oh, how I love that final taste of glory running as fast as I can over that line! As I crossed the finish that day, joy and a little relief rushed over me. By God's grace, I completed my first trail race. And I had learned a handful of life lessons along the way.

FAITH STEP: What are some of the things God has taught you while running? Are you experiencing any downhills or uphills in your life right now? In Psalm 27:11 David writes, "Teach me your way, LORD; lead me in a straight path." Make this verse the start of a prayer. Write out this verse and then add what you would say to God.

INSPIRATION: "Run when you can, walk if you have to, crawl if you must, just never give up."

—DEAN KARNAZES, American ultramarathoner

NOTES FROM COACH SHAWN: When running uphill during a race or long run, take shorter steps and pump your arms a little more. Think about lifting your knees with each stride during your ascent, and focus forward rather than down at your feet. On downhills, try not to lean back and land hard on your heels—that's like putting on the brakes. Instead, let your feet and legs roll underneath you with a faster cadence while maintaining control.

Use the space below to jot down some notes about your daily workouts or goals.

SUNDAY   MILES _____

MONDAY   MILES _____

TUESDAY   MILES _____

WEDNESDAY   MILES _____

THURSDAY   MILES _____

FRIDAY   MILES _____

SATURDAY   MILES _____

                                    TOTAL MILES _____

19

BUILDING SPIRITUAL MUSCLES

> She sets about her work vigorously; her arms are strong for
> her tasks.
>
> Proverbs 31:17

FAITH FUEL

Several months ago, a friend invited me to join her for a Sculpt class
at our local gym. I knew I needed to work on my cross-training,
so I agreed to go. She promised it would be a full-body workout,
and it would be hard. She was right.

The instructor, Jen, is a powerhouse. She expects 110 percent
effort and has the enthusiasm to help us soar. She creates unique,
high-intensity workouts, which include a combination of lifting
weights, core exercises, lunges, squats, cardio, and aerobic moves.
Jen presses play on the music and pushes us to work vigorously.
She doesn't like lots of downtime.

Sculpt is now a habit for me on Tuesday mornings. I don't have time in my schedule to take the class every day, but I use it as a day when I work intentionally to max out my muscles. Without someone pushing me, I'm more apt to skip a cross-training day and just go out and run.

Cross-training is important for runners and walkers because it helps us build our muscles. This gives us overall strength for running and durability, which protects us from injuries. If we have a strong core, it helps us hold our running form better and improves our breathing because we are not hunching over as much.

Lifting weights is especially important as we age. According to the *New York Times*, by our early forties, most of us are losing muscle mass at a rate of about 5 percent per decade.[1] Lifting weights or resistance training can slow down or reverse that descent. It can also help with motivation, mental sharpness, raising metabolism, and increasing mobility. Without resistance, our muscles atrophy or melt away as we age. Proverbs 31 includes an acrostic poem, which describes an ideal woman of strength and character. This passage of Scripture is used to encourage women to pursue the highest standards of excellence to please God. It doesn't say women need to be perfect, but it draws attention to the priorities, activities, character, and blessings women enjoy. Men can also study this passage to seek a wife of excellence or to encourage these qualities in the women in their lives.

Proverbs 31:17 describes a woman who is physically strong: "She sets about her work vigorously; her arms are strong for her tasks." I always think about this verse when I'm lifting weights and it feels hard. There's a purpose in weight training—it's so my arms will be strong for my daily tasks and running.

In Proverbs 31:25, we are reminded that strength is not just physical. We are to be women of character as well. The poem says, "She is clothed with strength and dignity; she can laugh at the days to come." We build spiritual strength and good character when we lift God's Word and rest in its truth. We need both in order to develop our spiritual muscles.

May we be men and women of strength who pivot away from physical and spiritual atrophy, and instead strengthen ourselves for the days to come.

FAITH STEP: If you don't already do this, schedule a regular time when you can do weight and core training this week. You might attend a class at a local gym, search for a home workout online, or go through the exercises described in the appendices of this devotional journal. Before or after your workout, plan to lift God's Word and read some Scripture as well.

INSPIRATION: "I think cross-country on the professional level plays to my strengths. On the track, where there are no obstacles and perfect conditions, it's harder to push people over the edge and break them. Cross-country allows a little more room for that kind of running."
—CHRIS DERRICK, 2013 USA cross-country champion

NOTES FROM COACH SHAWN: Regular strength training will improve your running posture and can help you run longer, faster, and injury-free. Focus on strengthening your core, which includes your abdomen, lower back, and hip flexors. Common core exercises include crunches, planks, leg scissors, and push-ups. Also include exercises for your calves, hamstrings, and glutes.

Use the space below to jot down some notes about your daily workouts or goals.

SUNDAY   MILES _____

MONDAY	MILES _____

TUESDAY	MILES _____

WEDNESDAY	MILES _____

THURSDAY	MILES _____

FRIDAY	MILES _____

SATURDAY	MILES _____

TOTAL MILES _____

20

SHOWING UP MATTERS

So we're not giving up. How could we! Even though on the outside it often looks like things are falling apart on us, on the inside, where God is making new life, not a day goes by without his unfolding grace.

2 Corinthians 4:16 MSG

FAITH FUEL

The announcer for the Miguel Reyes 5K race introduced the athletes. I watched in awe as the elite group lined up first. Each man and woman was unique—some tall, some short, some with shaved heads, some with long hair, but all with a similar lean frame and chiseled muscles. The rest of us fell into place behind them. The whistle sounded and we took off. This 5K course winds through the undulating dirt hills and green spaces of Woodward Park in Fresno, California. This is the same course that high-schoolers run for the state cross-country meet. As a coach and runner, I've traversed this course for many races, but I still felt out of place that morning.

I didn't have much get-up-and-go to tackle the hills or sprint it out at the finish. I slogged along and battled with my thoughts: "You're not in shape for this." "You are getting too old." "You're carrying too much weight these days." My forty-two-year-old body has birthed three baby girls and navigated a tough grief journey, among other things. I'm mushier around the middle. I look in the mirror and see laugh lines dancing around the corners of my eyes. My goals and focus have shifted. Now I run to clear my head. I run for therapy. I run to feel God's presence.

That day in the 5K race, God reminded me of something important: Showing up matters. Our goals may shift and our pace may wane, but we are still running. Your race isn't over until it's over. Being older and slower doesn't discount me from the race. In fact, maybe this is just the beginning. Maybe He's leading me down a new path to a new purpose in this season. A few years ago, a younger mama asked if I would mentor her. I paused at first because I didn't feel "old enough" to be a mentor. What wisdom did I have to offer? The more we chatted, the more I realized what she really wanted was someone to run alongside her in this race called life.

Now Yazmin and I set our eyes on the finish line together. Some days we run; other days we kneel. Finishing well and leading our people to God's glory is the goal. Friend, whether you are still raising babies or launching them out into the world, whether you are hoisting your broken body out of bed or speed-walking on a nearby trail, it still matters. Someone is watching you run your race, and your moving forward today could make all the difference. After the Miguel Reyes 5K race, I savored tacos, agua de Jamaica, and paletas with my daughters. I was sweaty and out of breath, stretching there on our red picnic blanket near the finish line. My seven-year-old looked up at me with her dark chocolate eyes and said, "Good job, Mama!" Another unexpected reminder that showing up still matters. We are teaching our baby birds how to fly.

FAITH STEP: Make a list of the people in your circle of influence who watch you run your life race. This might include your spouse, kids, parents, siblings, friends, or neighbors. Pray over this list and how you might make a positive impact on each one and their faith.

INSPIRATION: "Strong has never really been about how a body looks. It's about how a human lives. It's about lining up who we are inside with how we show up in the body we have."
    —LAUREN FLESHMAN, elite American distance runner

NOTES FROM COACH SHAWN: Volunteer at a local race at least once a year to give back to the running community. No race could be put on without volunteers. It also gives you a glimpse into the logistics of hosting an event and helps you appreciate all the work involved.

Use the space below to jot down some notes about your daily workouts or goals.

SUNDAY   MILES _____

MONDAY   MILES _____

TUESDAY   MILES _____

WEDNESDAY   MILES _____

THURSDAY   MILES _____

FRIDAY   MILES _____

SATURDAY   MILES _____

TOTAL MILES _____

21

COMING FULL CIRCLE

And God said, "I will be with you. And this will be the sign to you that it is I who have sent you: When you have brought the people out of Egypt, you will worship God on this mountain."

Exodus 3:12

FAITH FUEL

The conditions may not have been ideal for a race. Gray, overcast skies. Muddy, slippery trail. Of course, the elements rarely deter trail runners. They show up rain or shine for the pure adventure of the race.

My friend Heather and I donned running parkas and set out at the sound of the starting whistle. We were filled with gleeful anticipation of the race to come. I knew in my heart that God would show up with His presence and gift me some glimpse of His glory along the trail. He always does.

The first time I ran the San Joaquin River Gorge trail race was in 2015. That was my first trail race ever. Although I had been a runner all my life, I quickly discovered that running trails through hills and valleys was very different from racing on the flat road. Trails require negotiating rocks, ducking under tree branches, and sometimes coming face-to-face with wildlife.

That morning, the trail felt less intimidating. This was my third time running this race, and in many ways, I felt like I was coming full circle. We come full circle when we experience a series of developments or circumstances that lead us back to the original source, position, or situation. It feels like déjà vu but with a twist. Maybe you can relate.

In Exodus 3:12, God spoke to Moses from a burning bush. He promised to bring the people out of Egypt and that they would return to worship Him on Mount Sinai. This is the beginning of Moses' journey before he is sent out to rescue the Israelites from slavery and lead them to the promised land.

I imagine Moses felt like I did the first time I ran a trail race. I was unsure of my footing, tentative about what lay ahead, and insecure about my abilities to complete the race. In Exodus 19, Moses and the people finally escaped Egypt and journeyed back to the Desert of Sinai at the base of the mountain. Moses came full circle. Sometimes in life we have to return to the mountain so God can remind us who He is and set our feet back on the rock.

On that morning, God showed up for the Israelites in thunder and lighting, fire and smoke. God displayed just how big and powerful He is. He reminded them that He is greater than all the idols and false gods they could make for themselves. He underscored who He is—the Lord, the God of Israel—who is faithful to keep His covenant promises to them. He provided passage for them through the raging Red Sea and food for them in the desert.

Every time I go for a trail run, God shows me something new. One time He showed me His power in the rushing waterfall. Another time, He reminded me of His Presence through the fiery orange wings of a butterfly. On the San Joaquin River Trail, He renewed my courage on a familiar path. He helped me come full circle.

FAITH STEP: Are you coming full circle? Maybe you find yourself returning to a favorite childhood spot or connecting with an old friend. Maybe you are running the same race again or digging into some difficult memories from your past. If you are feeling like you are right back where you started, take heart. Take some time to reflect, and write down at least three things God has taught you on the journey.

INSPIRATION: "There is no major secret to success in athletics; the secret is the will. If you have the will to do it, then it will be possible."

—ELIUD KIPCHOGE, marathon world record holder

NOTES FROM COACH SHAWN: Run barefooted on grass to relive your childhood and to strengthen the muscles in your feet and lower legs. Start with only a couple of short strides and then gradually build up to a half mile. This often works well at the conclusion of a run.

Use the space below to jot down some notes about your daily workouts or goals.

SUNDAY   MILES _____

MONDAY   MILES _____

TUESDAY   MILES _____

WEDNESDAY   MILES _____

THURSDAY   MILES _____

FRIDAY   MILES _____

SATURDAY   MILES _____

TOTAL MILES _____

22

SOARING THROUGH
THE CLOUDS

And the LORD went before them by day in a pillar of cloud to
lead them along the way, and by night in a pillar of fire to give
them light, that they might travel by day and by night.

Exodus 13:21 ESV

FAITH FUEL

On my run yesterday, the clouds seemed to play hide-and-seek
with the sun. I loved those moments when the sun stood behind
the clouds and illuminated the edges. In the last several weeks,
we have experienced intermittent rains in central California. The
clouds often cause me to pause. Sometimes they are soft and bil-
lowy. Other times they are ominous, announcing a coming storm.

The clouds always remind me we serve a big, creative God who
is present with us. As we follow the journey of the Israelites in the
book of Exodus, I also can't help but marvel at the way God was

continually present with them. He rescues them from 430 years of slavery and brings them into new freedom. He goes before them as it says in Exodus 13:21, using a "pillar of cloud" and a "pillar of fire" to lead them through the desert to Mount Sinai.

Can you imagine the magnitude of a pillar of cloud that would guide thousands of Israelites by day and a pillar of fire that would light up the night sky to lead them through the dark desert? There were no headlamps, no flashlights, no phone lights, and no streetlamps to aid in this process—just God in all of His glory! God used His creation to command people's attention and to lead them.

Despite the Israelites' complaining and doubt, God was faithful to provide for them. He provided manna and quail when they were hungry. He offered them living water when they were thirsty. He gave them specific instructions about living in community, worship, building the tabernacle and the sanctuary. He showed them glimpses of His glory. He cared about every detail of their well-being—present and future.

Several times in Exodus, God reveals himself through the clouds. Exodus 24 describes when Moses met with God in a cloud: "When Moses went up on the mountain, the cloud covered it, and the glory of the LORD settled on Mount Sinai. For six days the cloud covered the mountain, and on the seventh day the LORD called to Moses from within the cloud" (Exodus 24:15–16). Moses goes into the cloud and stays with God there for forty days and forty nights. God shelters Moses and speaks to him in this hidden place.

God sometimes uses cloudy, uncertain times in our lives to draw us to himself. He may use clouds to invite us into His presence like He did with the Israelites. He often brings cooler temperatures on cloudy and overcast days. This can certainly be a relief from the heat when we are walking or running.

Friend, are you in the midst of a cloudy or rainy season? Are you spending too much time worrying about those dark storm clouds? Let me remind you today that He leads, speaks, and guides us through the clouds. He cares about the details of your life. You are never alone when you soar after God and His glory. He will illuminate your path.

FAITH STEP: How would you describe your life situation today? Is it cloudy or clear? Write in a journal or take some time to reflect here in these pages on how God might be using this season to draw you to himself.

INSPIRATION: "I'm not afraid to fail. I'll go toe the line even when I'm really tired in the middle of hard training. And a lot of times, I feel better than I think. . . ."

—SARA HALL, elite American marathoner

NOTES FROM COACH SHAWN: Motivate yourself to run by establishing a reward contingent upon your successfully accomplishing a specific goal. Consider setting a reward such as a new running outfit, a new pair of running socks, or even dinner out at your favorite restaurant.

Use the space below to jot down some notes about your daily workouts or goals.

SUNDAY   MILES _____

MONDAY   MILES _____

TUESDAY   MILES _____

WEDNESDAY   MILES _____

THURSDAY   MILES _____

FRIDAY   MILES _____

SATURDAY   MILES _____

TOTAL MILES _____

23

WALKING ON WATER

Then Peter called to him, "Lord, if it's really you, tell me
to come to you, walking on the water." "Yes, come," Jesus
said.

Matthew 14:28–29 NLT

FAITH FUEL

I trained for months for my second marathon. My friend Stacie got
up before dawn and rode a bike by my side while I ran my longest
runs. We chased the pastel colors of the sunrise and talked about
life. Her companionship and accountability were paramount. They
helped me get through the long miles, the early mornings, and
the heat.

On race day, I had to tackle the course alone. Stacie was not
allowed to ride her bike on the course, so she agreed to meet me
at the finish with my kids.

The Santa Rosa Marathon was especially appealing because
it was relatively flat. What I didn't anticipate was the camber of

the road. There was a slight angle to the pavement, which seemed subtle at first, but over many miles began to take its toll.

I started out strong, but by mile sixteen my right knee was screaming. With each step, a sharp pain reverberated. *This is bad,* I thought to myself. *This is really bad.* I made my way to the side of the street and tried to rest. A group of runners, who apparently had been pacing with me, called out, "Are you okay?"

"My knee is hurting," I answered with a weak smile. "I'm going to stretch it for a bit."

I bent over at the waist and pulled my right toes toward me in an effort to stretch. Then I straightened and continued on my way. The knee pain persisted. Discouragement began to rise in my spirit. I still had ten miles to go. Surely I couldn't turn back now. I started to break down mentally.

Another runner came up next to me. He noticed my slight limping and suggested I take smaller strides to put less stress on my knee. After a few minutes, he revealed that he was a doctor who ran ultramarathons. His advice helped, and I was on my way at a slower, steadier pace.

In Matthew 14, Jesus sends the disciples home in a boat as He dismisses the crowds and goes up on the mountain by himself to pray. A storm rises on the sea, and the disciples' boat is whipped by the wind. Jesus heads toward them, but He doesn't go by boat. *He walks on the water.*

"When the disciples saw him walking on the water, they were terrified. In their fear, they cried out, 'It's a ghost!'

"But Jesus spoke to them at once. 'Don't be afraid,' he said. 'Take courage. I am here!'" (Matthew 14:25–27 NLT).

The disciples found themselves in an unexpected storm. Their first response is fear, but Jesus gives them three important reminders: don't be afraid, take courage, and I am here. He is calling them out to have faith, courage, and trust in Him.

One of the disciples sees Jesus walking on the water and asks to join Him. "Yes, come," Jesus responds. "But when [Peter] saw the strong wind and the waves, he was terrified and began to sink. 'Save me, Lord!' he shouted. Jesus immediately reached out and rescued Peter" (Matthew 29-30 NLT).

When we keep our eyes on Jesus, instead of the wind and the waves, we can walk forward with confidence. Jesus meets us in the unexpected, in the storms, and even in the race when we are hurting.

I prayed all the way from mile sixteen to mile twenty-six of the Santa Rosa Marathon. Jesus granted me courage and saw me through. I soared across the finish line, which was nothing short of a miracle.

FAITH STEP: Have you ever had an injury or come up against an unexpected challenge? How did you respond? Maybe you are navigating stormy waters right now. Write out a prayer, shifting your trust and focus back on Jesus, who calms the storms and anchors us daily.

INSPIRATION: "I learned that courage was not the absence of fear, but the triumph over it. The brave man is not he who does not feel afraid, but he who conquers that fear."

—NELSON MANDELA, president of South Africa 1994–1999, and anti-apartheid leader

NOTES FROM COACH SHAWN: If you feel as if your heart rate begins to increase with no particular increase in effort, drink some water or electrolyte replacement fluid. This is often a sign that you are dehydrated.

Use the space below to jot down some notes about your daily workouts or goals.

SUNDAY   MILES

MONDAY   MILES _____

TUESDAY   MILES _____

WEDNESDAY   MILES _____

THURSDAY   MILES _____

FRIDAY   MILES _____

SATURDAY   MILES _____

TOTAL MILES _____

24

LOVING YOUR NEIGHBOR ON THE TRAIL

Jesus replied, "'You must love the Lord your God with all your heart, all your soul, and all your mind.' . . . A second is equally important: 'Love your neighbor as yourself.'"

Matthew 22:37, 39 NLT

FAITH FUEL

It's amazing how cooler weather can make me feel like I have wings. I had felt sluggish for much of the summer, but that morning I dropped off the kids and slipped out to run a 5K on the trail near my house. A gentle breeze kissed my shoulders as I fell into an easy pace.

I was fascinated by the diverse cross-section of people I passed. There was a mama pushing a toddler in a chariot stroller. A collective of older men in tunics conversed in another mother tongue. An attentive husband helped his pregnant wife with bulging belly walk gingerly down the path. A grandma pushed her granddaughter in a stroller while chatting with her daughter who walked by her side.

I couldn't help imagining the details of their stories. I tried to smile and say good morning to each person I passed. Maybe it was the cool air in my lungs or the angled light skipping across the path. Maybe it was the freedom to run free instead of sitting in the hot house. I felt inspired to reach out.

In the book of Matthew, Jesus is being challenged by a Pharisee. One of the men asks Jesus, "Teacher, which is the greatest commandment in the Law?" (Matthew 22:36).

Jesus replies, "'Love the Lord your God with all your heart and with all your soul and with all your mind.' This is the first and greatest commandment. And the second is like it: 'Love your neighbor as yourself.' All the Law and the Prophets hang on these two commandments" (Matthew 22:37–40).

In His response, Jesus groups these two fundamental commandments together and highlights how they are interconnected. The more we love God, the more we are compelled to love our neighbors. And the more we love our neighbors, the more we are driven to love God. One hinges upon the other. This is Old Testament wisdom meeting New Testament application. Jesus exemplified a balance between loving God and allowing that deep love to flow out as we love others.

In our American culture, we spend a lot of time with our eyes glued to our screens. It's common to ignore people around us even when we are out and about in the community. When running, we might pop in our earbuds, put our heads down, and just run. We can easily get stuck in our personal goals or problems.

What if God is calling you and me to lift our eyes on the trail? What if today you took the opportunity to show kindness and greet your neighbors as you walk, jog, or run? We are in this race called life together. Sometimes a simple wave or smile, acknowledging the other person as human, can make all the difference.

Some days I like to make it into a game. I try to say *hello, nice work*, or *good morning* to as many people as I can on the trail. The joy rises in me as their faces brighten and they respond.

Some people I pass regularly now. We recognize each other. We exchange a greeting or a head nod. Nothing fancy. Nothing extensive. There's something simply beautiful about sharing the same path and cheering each other on as we go.

FAITH STEP: Who are your "neighbors"? What does it look like to move out of your comfort zone to extend hospitality to someone in your community? Next time you are running or walking, try saying hello to someone you pass. Take the opportunity to encourage another runner on the trail.

INSPIRATION: "The secret is to make in your mind possible what was not possible before. The secret is to make easy what was difficult, instead to make difficult what really is easy."
   —RENATO CANOVA, famed coach of many of the top distance runners in the world

NOTES FROM COACH SHAWN: Motivate yourself to run by recruiting a running buddy who will keep you accountable to your running schedule, encourage you in your fitness goals, and is committed to meeting you for workouts.

Use the space below to jot down some notes about your daily workouts or goals.

SUNDAY   MILES

MONDAY   MILES

TUESDAY   MILES _____

WEDNESDAY   MILES _____

THURSDAY   MILES _____

FRIDAY   MILES _____

SATURDAY   MILES _____

TOTAL MILES _____

25

FRIEND AND FORERUNNER

"Truly, I say to you, among those born of women there has
arisen no one greater than John the Baptist. Yet the one who
is least in the kingdom of heaven is greater than he."

Matthew 11:11 ESV

FAITH FUEL

Some call him the GOAT (Greatest Of All Time). Others call him
Lightning Bolt. Usain Bolt solidified his place in Olympic history
at the games in Rio de Janeiro, Brazil, in 2016 when he snagged
the triple-triple. That meant the Jamaican-born superstar won
first place in the 100m, 200m, and 4x100m relay at three consecu-
tive Olympic games. Not to mention he's an eleven-time world
champion.

Bolt told CNN, "I am trying to be one of the greatest. Be among
Muhammad Ali and Pelé. I hope after these Games I will be in
that bracket."[1] Bolt was not satisfied with a few gold medals. He
had the drive and charisma to be the greatest athlete of all time.

Bolt garnered that title just before his thirtieth birthday. And no one in our present history can touch it.

In New Testament times, there was another GOAT. His name was John the Baptist. He was the friend and forerunner to Jesus Christ. The angel Gabriel describes John to his daddy, Zechariah, this way: "Your wife Elizabeth will bear you a son, and you are to call him John. He will be a joy and delight to you, and many will rejoice because of his birth, for he will be great in the sight of the Lord" (Luke 1:13). Talk about a cool vision for your son's future! And a geriatric pregnancy to boot!

A forerunner is a person who runs ahead or precedes the coming of someone else important. It's like a sign or warning, a precursor of something great to come. In distance races, the person who leads and sets the pace for the first section of runners is informally called the rabbit.

John and his mission were prophesied in Malachi 3:1, four hundred years before his birth. Like the prophets of old, John's life pointed to the Savior, but he had the added benefit of seeing Jesus face-to-face and walking with Him as a friend and disciple.

What is distinct about John is that he's a bold preacher, but he's also a humble guy who experiences doubt when he is in prison. "When John, who was in prison, heard about the deeds of the Messiah, he sent his disciples to ask him, 'Are you the one who is to come, or should we expect someone else?'" (Matthew 11:2–3). Jesus answers John's question indirectly by pointing to the miracles He was performing and the prophecy He had fulfilled. Jesus doesn't give His cousin preferential treatment. Instead, He forces John to reckon with his faith. And John knows right where to bring his doubts—to the feet of Jesus, the one he believes and eventually witnesses to be the Savior.

Jesus goes on to affirm John as the GOAT to the crowds in Matthew 11:11: "Truly, I say to you, among those born of women there has arisen no one greater than John the Baptist. Yet the one who is least in the kingdom of heaven is greater than he" (ESV).

Jesus affirms who he is, but He also makes clear that the last shall be first in His kingdom.

John is a forerunner. He is born with and follows a clear life purpose—to lead people to be disciples of Jesus Christ. This was his calling. And this is our calling as well. The goal is not to be the greatest of all time and win all the glory for ourselves, but to point others to the One who is to come and His glory.

FAITH STEP: Is there an area in which you have been striving for personal glory? How can you shift your perspective so you might also point people to Jesus like John did? Write down a few ways you can give God glory through your walking or running this week.

INSPIRATION: "You can't go for a world record thinking, 'Oh, I'm going to be careful, I'm only going 80 percent.' That doesn't work. It's a world record for a reason so you have to give everything you have. Despite what might happen later."

—2016 Olympic high-jump silver medalist MUTAZ ESSA BARSHIM on rupturing his ankle ligaments while attempting a world record

NOTES FROM COACH SHAWN: Before every run you should identify the goal of the workout. The goal may be to run a specific pace, work on your leg turnover, develop power, or simply have the freedom to run easy and enjoy the scenery. At the completion of a run, evaluate whether or not you attained your goal.

Use the space below to jot down some notes about your daily workouts or goals.

SUNDAY   MILES _____

MONDAY   MILES _____

TUESDAY   MILES _____

WEDNESDAY   MILES _____

THURSDAY   MILES _____

FRIDAY   MILES _____

SATURDAY   MILES _____

TOTAL MILES _____

26

RUNNING FOR DIAMONDS

Dear friends, do not be surprised at the fiery ordeal that has
come on you to test you, as though something strange were
happening to you. But rejoice inasmuch as you participate in
the sufferings of Christ, so that you may be overjoyed when
his glory is revealed.

1 Peter 4:12–13

FAITH FUEL

We gathered at the starting line, donning our turquoise race tank
tops with the signature "run smile" logo. Women of all ages,
shapes, and sizes buzzed with excitement to run the Diamond 10K
in my hometown of Fresno, California. My friend Sunny, owner
and founder of the running apparel and jewelry company Endure,
hosted the race as a celebration of the tenth anniversary of her
company. One of the biggest draws for runners was the diamond
necklace they awarded each competitor at the finish line, instead
of the traditional medal.

The community of (mostly) women who came out to run was friendly and encouraging. We cheered and high-fived each other along the trail. For the first three miles of the race, I felt great. I was clipping along at a faster-than-usual pace.

Then I got to mile four, and the sun started beating down on my shoulders. The sweat started to chase down my back. Just looking ahead at the dusty trail made me feel thirsty. Partway through mile four I was at the base of Killer Hill. You can probably imagine why they call it Killer Hill. It's a doozy, especially when you're already hot and slowing down. I decided to put one foot in front of the other and pump my arms.

Once, I read in *Smithsonian* magazine that diamonds are formed about a hundred miles below the earth's surface, where it's extremely hot and there's high pressure. The combination of pressure and heat is what's necessary to create diamond crystals. This race was appropriately called the Diamond 10K.

Despite the heat on Sunday, I was determined. After all, a diamond necklace was at stake! (Not to mention sparkly-sprinkle donuts, a massage, a yoga class, and ice cream, which were all promised at the finish line!) I sprinted across the finish line at the hour mark.

The women I saw finish on Sunday had their own diamond stories—beautiful, resilient, and multifaceted. I was struck that God often uses heat and pressure to form the gems of our character. He reveals His glory through the trials.

In the Bible, Peter encourages believers to have endurance through suffering and trials. He reminds us not to be surprised by the heat and pressure: "Dear friends, do not be surprised at the fiery ordeal that has come on you to test you, as though something strange were happening to you. But rejoice inasmuch as you participate in the sufferings of Christ, so that you may be overjoyed when his glory is revealed" (1 Peter 4:12–13).

Do you feel like you are in the midst of the fire right now? Maybe you are facing challenges at work or in a relationship. Maybe you are feeling the financial strain or waiting on direction for your future. Friend, perhaps you are living a diamond story too. It's uncomfortable in the heat and trials, but the result is beauty that can reflect God's glory to the world like diamonds.

FAITH STEP: Are you coming up on a surprising Killer Hill in your life? Is there an area where you feel like you're facing the heat? Write out 1 Peter 4:12–13 on a note card and hang it in a prominent place where you will see it—like your car dashboard, on your bathroom mirror, or over the kitchen sink.

INSPIRATION: "You can keep going and your legs might hurt for a week, or you can quit and your mind will hurt for a lifetime."

—MARK ALLEN, six-time Ironman world champion

NOTES FROM COACH SHAWN: In a race, sometimes it is helpful to disassociate yourself from your running for short periods. Focus on anything but your running or the pain and discomfort. Focus on the scenery, dream about the future, think about your favorite movie, or anything else to give your mind a short break.

Use the space below to jot down some notes about your daily workouts or goals.

SUNDAY   MILES

MONDAY   MILES

TUESDAY   MILES

WEDNESDAY   MILES _____

THURSDAY   MILES _____

FRIDAY   MILES _____

SATURDAY   MILES _____

TOTAL MILES _____

27

SUITING UP WITH PROPER GEAR

Therefore put on the full armor of God, so that when the day of evil comes, you may be able to stand your ground, and after you have done everything, to stand.

Ephesians 6:13

FAITH FUEL

One weekend we were visiting my brother and his family in Southern California. At the time, I was training for the Shadow of the Giants 20K trail race. I knew at least the first five miles of the race would be winding uphill, so I needed to put in some hill training. My brother suggested we train on the Claremont Loop at Claremont Hills Wilderness Park. My hubby-coach, Shawn, agreed this would be a great place to get in my long miles before race day. The loop is approximately five miles, so we aimed to run it twice.

After several years of trail running, I have learned the importance of dressing properly to run long miles. Running is not like other sports that require loads of expensive gear, but suiting up properly can make or break an experience, especially if it involves longer distances or more technical terrains. Shawn says it's always important to try out gear before race day.

Shoes are of primary importance. A good pair of trail shoes with extra ventilation and traction make a world of difference on a rocky or muddy path. Specially designed trail socks also help prevent blisters. I look for trail socks that dry quickly just in case my feet get wet, which happens frequently.

As a runner, we learn to check the weather first. This helps determine if I will wear shorts, tights, tank top, a long-sleeved outer layer, rain parka, etc. I always run with sunglasses, a hydration pack or water bottle, my phone for safety and photos, and Honey Stinger chews for fuel during the run. I'm sure you have your go-to gear as well.

My trail shoes dug into the red earth of the Claremont Loop trail while a misty rain continued to moisten the ground. My sunglasses were not protection from the sun that day; instead, they were a shield from the rain. I was prepared. I couldn't help thinking about the passage in Ephesians where Paul calls believers to get ready for battle and put on the full armor of God. He wanted them to be prepared and properly outfitted for the attacks of the forces of evil.

In Ephesians 6, Paul makes a comparison between the physical armor used for battle and the spiritual gear needed to fight the tactics of the enemy. He urges readers to "Stand firm then, with the belt of truth buckled around your waist, with the breastplate of righteousness in place, and with your feet fitted with the readiness that comes from the gospel of peace. In addition to all this, take up the shield of faith, with which you can extinguish all the flaming arrows of the evil one. Take the helmet of salvation and the sword of the Spirit, which is the word of God" (Ephesians 6:14–17).

Paul was writing from prison to the believers in the church at Ephesus, which was the capital of the Roman province of Asia. This letter would circulate to the other churches in Asia Minor. This is significant because Paul wanted all of them (and all of us reading today) to be battle-ready. He knew the devil was the enemy and he would attack when we are most vulnerable.

Friend, do you suit up for spiritual battles like you do for a race? Let's slip into God's armor daily so together we can move forward in faith, strength, and peace as Paul describes.

FAITH STEP: Read Ephesians 6:10–20 aloud before your next long run or walk. Imagine yourself putting on the various parts of "armor" that Paul describes. Pray as you run for "all the Lord's people" (Ephesians 6:18).

INSPIRATION: "Your body will argue that there is no justifiable reason to continue. Your only recourse is to call on your spirit, which fortunately functions independently of logic."

—DR. TIM NOAKES, expert on running and exercise science

NOTES FROM COACH SHAWN: A critical thing that you should take with you on every run is personal identification in case there is an emergency. Road iD, for example, makes customized bracelets that runners can wear with their name, contact information, medication, allergies, and any existing health conditions.

Use the space below to jot down some notes about your daily workouts or goals.

SUNDAY   MILES _____

MONDAY   MILES _____

TUESDAY   MILES _____

WEDNESDAY   MILES _____

THURSDAY   MILES _____

FRIDAY   MILES _____

SATURDAY   MILES _____

                                       TOTAL MILES _____

28

VALUING THE
BUILDING PROCESS

Unless the LORD builds the house, those who build it labor in vain. Unless the LORD watches over the city, the watchman stays awake in vain.

Psalm 127:1 ESV

FAITH FUEL

Up the running trail from my house, they're building a slew of new condos and houses. That means the trail is full of dust and debris, construction cones redirecting us, and barricades protecting us from dangers. Through the days and weeks, I am watching the process of building these new homes. First, the foundations are laid. Then the frame of the house or apartment is put up. Next, builders install windows and doors, roofing, siding, and drywall. Finally, the important details go in, like electrical, plumbing, flooring, and paint. When I train for a race, Shawn typically helps me build a training plan based on my goals and time to work out. Training is the building process for runners and walkers. It's where our fitness foundation is built and our character is forged. When we build and follow a training plan, we are more prepared for surprises and ready for race day.

In training for a race, I'm disciplining my body and my mind. I need to be committed to training, which helps me build strength, stamina, and speed over time. I might start out training for a half marathon or marathon by running only a few miles and increasing my distance each week. Shawn often has me add in core exercises and weight lifting to help prevent injuries and tempo runs to build up speed.

As runners and in life, we need to have a "growth mindset," which thrives on challenge and sees failure as a catalyst for growth. This helps us stretch beyond our existing abilities. A hard training day helps build resilience in us so we can take on the challenge of the longest distances. In many races, I find myself recalling the hardest training days to help give myself that pep talk I need to get to the finish line.

Psalm 127:1 says that unless the Lord builds a house, its builders labor in vain. In other words, without the blessing and guidance of the Lord, our human efforts are worthless. We need to trust and depend on God to be the foreman of anything we build. Otherwise, we are seeking glory for ourselves. He can guide the building process and grow our character along the way.

I feel like there's a lot under construction in my life right now. Maybe you feel it in yours too. We are staring down a lot of transition at work, school, home, and church. I was reminded this morning that construction is an important part of the process. It's messy and hard, but it's required before we can live in that new house, work at a new job, run a new race, or transition into a new context. I'm learning not to shy away from demolition, construction, and the building process.

Friends, let's retrain our hearts to be thankful for the 2x4s on the path, for the dust on our running shoes, and for the sun rising before us—all reminders that He is at work building new things.

FAITH STEP: What is under construction in your life right now? How can you pivot away from doing things on your own and let God build in new ways in your life? Take some time to draw a sketch of what God is building. Label the foundation, the walls, windows, doors, etc. What steps do you need to take to follow God's plan?

INSPIRATION: "You need three things to win: discipline, hard work, and, before everything, maybe commitment. No one will make it without those three. Sport teaches you that."

—HAILE GEBRSELASSIE, Ethiopian distance runner and former world-record holder

NOTES FROM COACH SHAWN: Set new running goals for the New Year and select the races you want to focus on so you can develop a yearlong training schedule. An effective training schedule incorporates a mix of hard workouts and recovery. It will have different weekly and monthly cycles to focus on mileage, speed, and recovery.

Use the space below to jot down some notes about your daily workouts or goals.

SUNDAY	MILES

MONDAY	MILES

TUESDAY	MILES

WEDNESDAY   MILES _____

THURSDAY   MILES _____

FRIDAY   MILES _____

SATURDAY   MILES _____

                                    TOTAL MILES _____

29

BATTLING FEAR
ON THE COURSE

> Therefore, I remind you to keep ablaze the gift of God that
> is in you through the laying on of my hands. For God has not
> given us a spirit of fearfulness, but one of power, love, and
> sound judgment.
>
> 2 Timothy 1:6–7 HCSB

FAITH FUEL

When I set out for a run this morning, I was greeted by ominous fog. I could see only a few steps in front of me on the path. I didn't know what I would face ahead. I couldn't anticipate any curves or hills or other people along the path. My mind began to race with the fear of the unknown.

I've been battling with fear these last few weeks. My mind keeps returning to fears of my kids getting deathly sick, school shootings, or another cancer diagnosis for a loved one. The fears even build up in my running life when I am fearful of getting injured, getting sick, or not having enough stamina to get to the finish line. Then there is the fear of failure, rejection, and shame that creeps into our lives and thoughts. Sometimes I sit with the fear of what might happen if I step out in obedience to where God is leading me.

I don't know about you, but I can make myself sick with worry and anxiety if I focus on all there is to fear. When we let fear overtake us and put us in the corner cowering, we may never step into our calling. We may never experience the abundance God has for us each day.

The apostle Paul wrote a letter to Timothy, who was like his dearly loved son in the faith. He wrote to encourage Timothy in his role as a pastor. Second Timothy 1:6–7 serves as an exhortation to Timothy to keep his spiritual gift alive. Paul writes, "Therefore, I remind you to keep ablaze the gift of God that is in you through the laying on of my hands. For God has not given us a spirit of fearfulness, but one of power, love, and sound judgment" (HCSB). God's Word says to "keep ablaze the gift" He gives us and not to hold back because of fear and timidity.

When I was a little girl, I used to be afraid of the dark. My mama made me memorize 2 Timothy 1:7. She trained me to recite these words aloud whenever I was afraid. As I would repeat the words "power, love, and sound mind" the courage would rise up in me. We can do the same today. Let's turn our focus away from fear and toward faith in what God has given us.

When you are running through the fog of life, shift your perspective and determine to put your eyes on what is right in front of you instead of on the fog much farther down the road. Soon, that fog will lift and you will have space to soar again.

FAITH STEP: Write down three fears you might be facing in your everyday life or your training. Then cross out those fears and replace them with praise and gratitude to God for what He has given you in this season.

INSPIRATION: "I never pray to God to help me win. I pray to be ready, healthy, give my best. I pray against fear, because fear kills promise. Fear makes you focus on the other athletes, not yourself. Fear makes you want the bathroom, makes your head hurt."

—SHELLY-ANN FRASER-PRYCE, Jamaican Olympic gold medalist sprinter

NOTES FROM COACH SHAWN: Before each race, preview the course by running it beforehand, paying attention to turns and hills. Also make note of any camber in the road, potholes, and areas of shade. Knowing what to expect will alleviate some pre-race nerves and fears about the course.

Use the space below to jot down some notes about your daily workouts or goals.

SUNDAY	MILES

MONDAY	MILES

TUESDAY	MILES

WEDNESDAY	MILES

THURSDAY	MILES

FRIDAY   MILES _____

SATURDAY   MILES _____

                                   TOTAL MILES _____

30

HONORING OUR
SACRED BODIES

Or didn't you realize that your body is a sacred place, the place of the Holy Spirit? Don't you see that you can't live however you please, squandering what God paid such a high price for? The physical part of you is not some piece of property belonging to the spiritual part of you. God owns the whole works. So let people see God in and through your body.

1 Corinthians 6:19–20 MSG

FAITH FUEL

As the mother of three girls, I'm acutely aware they are watching and listening. The way I treat my body, talk about my body, and display my body influences the way they regard their bodies. As my friend Maria Furlough writes, "We are the confidence standards in our homes. We set the tone and the example of what confidence looks like."[1] I long to take them under my wing and model godly, humble confidence for them.

We all have to daily process the images and perceptions of beauty portrayed on television and social media, in books and magazines, and even among friends. Many of these images paint beauty in a singular way that no one could ever live up to or emulate. That's why I am careful with the language I use in my home and among my girls. We don't talk about things like diets, fat, or BMI. We talk about healthy choices, not weight loss.

On the other hand, it's common for runners—both male and female—to obsess about calories and weight. There is a whole different standard in the running community. We tell ourselves things like, "I ate the chocolate cake, now I need to go run." But some off-the-cuff comments and "humorous" T-shirt slogans can spiral into damaging negative self-talk or eating disorders if we are not careful. I am challenged to turn to God's Word for wisdom.

In 1 Corinthians, Paul writes to the church of Corinth on many controversial topics of the day. Corinth was a thriving Roman colony, which hosted a transient population because of trade. Corinth was also a city with notable ethnic, cultural, religious, and economic diversity. Paul is compassionate yet firm on issues of immorality and pride. In 1 Corinthians 6:18 he specifically says, "Run from sexual immorality!" (HCSB). He goes on to explain that sexual sin is actually sin against our own bodies.

Then Paul challenges and exhorts his audience: "Or didn't you realize that your body is a sacred place, the place of the Holy Spirit? Don't you see that you can't live however you please, squandering what God paid such a high price for? The physical part of you is not some piece of property belonging to the spiritual part of you. God owns the whole works. So let people see God in and through your body" (1 Corinthians 6:19-20 MSG).

Paul's words challenge us to think about our bodies from a new perspective. During the time Paul writes, one of the slogans of the Corinthians was "Everything is permissible for me." In other words, there were very few standards. Paul responds with this concept that our bodies are a sacred place or a home for the Holy Spirit.

If our bodies are home to the Holy Spirit, you and I should be more intentional about exercise and food because this body is like rental property; it doesn't belong to us. Let's work to treat our bodies with more love, respect, and grace. Paul concludes with, "You were bought with a price. Therefore honor God with your bodies." The way we view and treat our bodies privately and publicly provides us an opportunity to bring God glory.

FAITH STEP: In 1 Corinthians 10:31, Paul writes, "So whether you eat or drink or whatever you do, do it all for the glory of God." Our purpose is to glorify God with our bodies. How can you bring Him glory in the way you train, rest, eat, and worship? Write down some goals in each of these areas. Share with a friend for accountability.

INSPIRATION: "If you have a body, you are an athlete."

—BILL BOWERMAN, legendary track-and-field coach for the University of Oregon (1948–1972) and co-founder of Nike

NOTES FROM COACH SHAWN: Take care of your body. Incorporate cross-training—weights, cycling, swimming, aerobics—into your training schedule to improve overall fitness. Stretching and yoga are fantastic ways to keep your muscles limber and reduce the likelihood of injury.

Use the space below to jot down some notes about your daily workouts or goals.

SUNDAY   MILES _____

MONDAY   MILES _____

TUESDAY   MILES _____

WEDNESDAY   MILES _____

THURSDAY   MILES _____

FRIDAY   MILES _____

SATURDAY   MILES _____

TOTAL MILES _____

31

YOUR RACE ISN'T OVER YET

So we're not giving up. How could we! Even though on the outside it often looks like things are falling apart on us, on the inside, where God is making new life, not a day goes by without his unfolding grace.

2 Corinthians 4:16 MSG

FAITH FUEL

I've been running with my daddy since I was a little girl. The first race we ran together was the Ridge Run 10K on the south side of Chicago near the neighborhood where I grew up. More than three thousand runners gather each year to run this 10K on Memorial Day, followed by a parade. Neighbors line the course to cheer and play motivating music for the runners. The course runs along Longwood Drive and includes running up one of the steepest hills in Chicago before runners continue on to the finish.

Dad helped me train for this race by taking me out for jogs in our neighborhood. While we ran, he taught me about breathing and pacing. He talked to me about building up our strength and stamina for race day. We knew eight city blocks equaled a mile. Dad would map out our mileage before we ran. Some days those miles felt long to my nine-year-old legs. Even if I was tired, he wouldn't let me stop. He would urge me to just keep moving forward.

The apostle Paul wrote these encouraging words to the church at Corinth: "So we're not giving up. How could we! Even though on the outside it often looks like things are falling apart on us, on the inside, where God is making new life, not a day goes by without his unfolding grace" (2 Corinthians 4:16 MSG).

Paul reveals a key to the Christian life that we can be renewed daily in our spirits because of God's unfolding grace. This affects our bodies too, enabling us to keep going even when we feel tired, worn out, and old. This was an important message for the Christians living in Corinth because they were facing false teachers and discouragement. Paul reminds them that their current troubles were achieving for them an eternal glory. This is a powerful reminder for us too. You and I will face trials on earth, but we will experience God's glory and be rewarded in heaven.

I treasured those times running with my dad. Now my dad is seventy-seven years old, and he's still running 5Ks, 10Ks, and the occasional half marathon. He has faithfully run and raised thousands of dollars for our Remember Haiti fundraiser team for the last decade. Dad's legs are slower, his breathing is heavier, and he struggles with sciatica, but he won't stop. In fact, he's made it to the podium several times to get awards in his seventy-plus age group.

A few years ago the doctor told my dad to stop running races. He urged him to walk. Of course, it's tough to get an old man to stop doing something he's done all his life. Sometimes I would catch him running out on the track or on the course. I'd lovingly scold him. He'd laugh and promise he would walk. Sure enough, I'd catch him jogging again later. His perseverance—or perhaps persistence—is admirable.

Friend, we are not promised tomorrow, but if we are still living today, our race isn't over. My dad serves as my constant inspiration. We all have to keep running this race set before us for God's glory.

FAITH STEP: Is there an area in your training or your life where you feel like giving up? What would it look like for you to persevere through this? Share your goal or situation with a trusted friend or running buddy and ask them to pray for you.

INSPIRATION: "Dreams are free. Goals have a cost. While you can daydream for free, goals don't come without a price. Time, effort, sacrifice, and sweat. How will you pay for your goals?"

—USAIN BOLT, Jamaican world-record holder in the 100m and 200m

NOTES FROM COACH SHAWN: Don't underestimate the importance of your arms—they keep your legs moving. The faster you move your arms, the faster your legs will move. This is critical in the later stages of a race as fatigue sets in. Keep your shoulders relaxed and keep your arms swinging.

Use the space below to jot down some notes about your daily workouts or goals.

SUNDAY	MILES

MONDAY	MILES

TUESDAY   MILES _____

WEDNESDAY   MILES _____

THURSDAY   MILES _____

FRIDAY   MILES _____

SATURDAY   MILES _____

TOTAL MILES _____

32

WALKING LIKE JESUS

By this we may know that we are in him: whoever says he abides in him ought to walk in the same way in which he walked.

1 John 2:5–6 ESV

FAITH FUEL

My knee screamed every time I put weight on it. I decided to take the entire week off running and tried a new chiropractor. Dr. Tsutsui found that a rolled ankle was causing big stress to my left knee. He also discovered a pinched nerve in my back that had likely caused the numbness in my left foot for the past six months. In addition, I had a rib out of place, which explained my right shoulder pain. Needless to say, I was grateful for some pain relief.

However, this meant I really had to take recovery seriously—prioritizing rest, staying off the trails on weekends, and nourishing well. Sometimes our bodies force us to prune back and rest when we put too much stress on them over time. Admittedly, I felt a little sorry for myself when all my mama friends were headed out to chase some glory in the mountains.

Finally, with my doctor's blessing and strict orders to stay on flat ground, I was able to drag myself out for a slow run/walk. I was bummed to go by myself, but God is always faithful to meet me in the quiet. He reminded me of the value in walking with Him at His pace. There are times to sprint. There are times to press uphill. And there are times to steal away with Him and rest. I didn't have to go hunting for beauty in the hills. He offered it to me through the sweet pink blooms right on the corner near my house.

First John 2:6 reads, "Whoever says he abides in him ought to walk in the same way in which he walked." John wrote for the congregations in Asia Minor to remind us today to walk like Jesus walked. Jesus deliberately chose to walk shoulder-to-shoulder with people. He was the King, but He did not travel in a chariot or ride a majestic horse like other kings of His time. He didn't ride around town in a Tesla or a limousine. He walked. He invites each of us to follow Him.

Colossians 1:10 gives us some clues about how to walk like Jesus. While imprisoned in Rome, Paul wrote this letter and prayed over the believers of the church of Colossae that they might "walk in a manner worthy of the Lord." He prayed that they would be filled with wisdom and understanding of God's will, that they might be fully pleasing to God, and that they would bear fruit in every good work. He wanted them to be confident in their faith and to understand they had freedom in Christ. His love did not need to be earned. He simply wanted to link arms and walk down the dusty path with them day by day.

After a horrible death on the cross, Jesus walked out of the grave, and then eventually soared to heaven. When we believe in Him and walk with Him, we have freedom from the sin that weighs us down. We can enjoy regular rest in Him. And we have the opportunity to soar to heaven one day to be with Him for eternity.

FAITH STEP: What would it look like for you to walk like Jesus? Are you running too hard, despite your injuries? Is He calling you to stop striving and start abiding in Him? Write God a letter today about what you need to surrender so you might walk in freedom and restoration.

INSPIRATION: "The idea that the harder you work, the better you're going to be is just garbage. The greatest improvement is made by the man or woman who works most intelligently."

—BILL BOWERMAN, legendary track-and-field coach for the University of Oregon (1948–1972) and co-founder of Nike

NOTES FROM COACH SHAWN: When preparing for a race, it is better to be 10 percent undertrained than 10 percent overtrained. Overtraining often results in injuries, severe and chronic fatigue, and/or a consistently much higher than normal resting heart rate, and your performance on race day will be worse than if you are a little undertrained.

Use the space below to jot down some notes about your daily workouts or goals.

SUNDAY   MILES

MONDAY   MILES

TUESDAY   MILES

WEDNESDAY   MILES

THURSDAY	MILES _____

FRIDAY	MILES _____

SATURDAY	MILES _____

TOTAL MILES _____

33

LETTING GOD NOURISH US

The angel of the Lord came back a second time and touched him and said, "Get up and eat, for the journey is too much for you." So he got up and ate and drank. Strengthened by that food, he traveled forty days and forty nights until he reached Horeb, the mountain of God.

1 Kings 19:7–8

FAITH FUEL

After running my first 20K trail race, I remember crossing the finish line with a huge sense of accomplishment. I was both exhausted and ravenous. The race director pointed us to the dining area, where they provided water, snacks, fruit, and soup for the runners. That's right, soup! The noodles and thick chunks of chicken swirled in my bowl with the carrots, celery, and onions. I dug in. The salty taste tickled my tongue. I had never eaten a hearty bowl of chicken noodle soup after an endurance race before, but it turned out to be just the nourishment my body needed.

That bowl of soup is almost iconic in my mind today as I think about how amazing it tasted and how it warmed my bones after that challenging race. I've run in other races with fabulous eats at the finish line—street tacos, sparkly donuts, pancakes, eggs, sausage, bacon, or breakfast burritos—but none of these quite topped the chicken noodle soup.

In the same way that soup nourished my body, God longs to nourish us. But He goes above and beyond chicken noodle soup. He nourishes our bodies, minds, and souls. God's provision for us is personal and powerful. One of my favorite examples of this is illustrated in 1 Kings. This book is written for the Jewish exiles throughout Assyria and Babylon during the time of King Solomon's rule, and points people to the only true God—Yahweh, who keeps His covenant to the people despite their unfaithfulness.

In 1 Kings 18, the prophet Elijah goes up against Ahab, Jezebel, and the prophets of Baal. If you aren't familiar with this dramatic story, Elijah stands on Mount Carmel and displays the power of Yahweh, who sends down fire before all the people. Then all the prophets of Baal are slaughtered. The power of God is displayed through Elijah.

Despite being used by God for this miracle, Elijah shows he is still human when he falls subject to exhaustion, despair, and depression after this intense time of serving God. Queen Jezebel sends Elijah a threatening message. Elijah feared for his life and ran into the wilderness to hide. He cried out to God. "I have had enough, LORD," he said. "Take my life; I am no better than my ancestors" (1 Kings 19:4). Then Elijah lay down and fell asleep.

An angel of the Lord found him there and offered him just what he needed: rest and nourishment. The passage says the angel of the Lord came and touched Elijah and brought him hot bread and fresh water. Elijah slept some more.

"Then angel of the LORD came back a second time and touched him and said, 'Get up and eat, for the journey is too much for you.' So he got up and ate and drank. Strengthened by that food, he traveled forty days and forty nights until he reached Horeb, the mountain of God" (1 Kings 19:7–8). Maybe it's because I'm a foodie, but I am deeply moved by the way God provides delicious, hot bread and fresh water for Elijah in his time of need. (Talk about some serious superfood. That stuff sustained Elijah for forty days and nights on a journey he was too tired to begin!) God gives Elijah permission to rest and encouragement for the journey.

Friend, let this story encourage you that God doesn't care about just our physical needs or just our spiritual needs. He cares deeply about both. We can try to nourish ourselves or we can trust God, who knows our deepest needs and longs to provide for all of them.

FAITH STEP: Nutrition is important for runners and walkers. What kinds of foods do you eat to nourish yourself before, during, and after a race? Take some time to write down what helps energize you or what doesn't sit well with you. What are some of the ways you allow God to nourish you spiritually? Maybe it's reading your Bible, memorizing Scripture, attending a small group, or something else. If you haven't engaged in some of these practices before, make it a goal to make one or more part of your daily routine.

INSPIRATION: "Stepping outside the comfort zone is the price I pay to find out how good I can be."
  —DESIREE LINDEN, 2018 Boston Marathon champion

NOTES FROM COACH SHAWN: After a run, quickly replenish the fluids you lost through sweat during the run. Also, your body is most ready to absorb nutrients during a thirty-minute window following exercise, so eat some protein and carbohydrates to help your recovery process.

Use the space below to jot down some notes about your daily workouts or goals.

SUNDAY   MILES _____

MONDAY   MILES _____

TUESDAY   MILES _____

WEDNESDAY   MILES _____

THURSDAY   MILES _____

FRIDAY   MILES _____

SATURDAY   MILES _____

TOTAL MILES _____

34

HITTING THE WALL

I waited patiently for the LORD to help me, and he turned to me and heard my cry. He lifted me out of the pit of despair, out of the mud and the mire. He set my feet on solid ground and steadied me as I walked along. He has given me a new song to sing, a hymn of praise to our God.

Psalm 40:1–3

FAITH FUEL

Several years ago I was running the Two Cities Half Marathon in Fresno with our Remember Haiti team. For most of the 13.1 miles I ran on my own and felt great. I enjoyed the flat course, the trail that ran through beautiful corridors of fiery-colored trees, and the local fans cheering us on. However, around mile ten, I hit the proverbial wall.

My shoulders started to droop. I could feel the crust of salt lining my cheeks. My breathing was uneven. My legs felt heavy. I imagined myself running through a huge vat of molasses getting nowhere fast.

Scientific studies have shown that "hitting the wall" is a common thing among distance runners. Hitting the wall (or bonking) is the feeling of sudden fatigue and loss of energy caused by the depletion of glycogen stores in the liver and muscles. Even the brain shuts down as a preservation method when bonking, which could lead to negative and defeated thinking. Many marathoners hit the wall around miles eighteen to twenty, while half-marathoners may bonk around miles ten or eleven.

This sinking feeling rises up in your gut. You know you've run too far to turn around, but you're unsure if you have the energy to get to the finish line. Lots of runners slow down and battle discouragement at this point.

In that Two Cities Half Marathon, I was struggling at mile ten. I was alone on the course. There weren't many fans cheering on that particular stretch. I felt tired and suddenly emotional. I was seriously thinking about walking the rest of the way. Then a guy ran up next to me. He was a friend I hadn't seen in years. Karl and I started chatting, and he admitted that he was hitting the wall too. We laughed and decided to get through to the finish line together.

When David, in the Bible, hit the wall, he cried out to God. I love his honest words in Psalm 40:1: "I waited patiently for the LORD to help me, and he turned to me and heard my cry" (NLT). The important part is God's response to David, which he describes in the following verses: "He lifted me out of the pit of despair, out of the mud and the mire. He set my feet on solid ground and steadied me as I walked along. He has given me a new song to sing, a hymn of praise to our God" (Psalm 40:2 NLT).

God did three key things: He rescued David from the pit; He steadied his feet on a firm foundation; and He gave him a new song to sing. This lifted David's spirits and helped him shift his attitude so he could keep running his race.

Friend, maybe you're right up against that wall today in your life. Maybe you're battling depression, anxiety, or fear about the future. Maybe your marriage is falling apart or you are watching your child struggle and you don't know how to help him. Maybe you are in a season of waiting and you feel like you are running but getting nowhere fast. It's okay to cry out to God like David did. He hears our cries and can put a new song in our heart.

As Karl and I ran the final few miles of the Two Cities Half Marathon, something shifted in my heart too. I returned to the truth that I had trained well for this race, and I could finish with God's help. I put one foot in front of the other and ran. Shawn was at the finish line announcing the finishers' names. Great joy welled up in my heart as I heard him say my name.

FAITH STEP: Have you ever "hit the wall" in a training run or race? What about in your personal or spiritual life? Do you feel a sense of urgency like David did? Cry out to God today and ask Him for help. Write out a prayer or pray as you run.

INSPIRATION: "The real purpose of running isn't to win a race; it's to test the limits of the human heart."

—BILL BOWERMAN, legendary track-and-field coach for the University of Oregon (1948–1972) and co-founder of Nike

NOTES FROM COACH SHAWN: If you begin to hit the wall in running, immediately hydrate with an electrolyte sports drink and consume some carbohydrates in the form of sports gels, energy chews, or pretzels. The fuel will help perk you up and will hopefully provide you a second wind. If you are in a race and are healthy enough to continue, keep putting one step in front of the other and focus only on getting to the next mile marker. Don't worry about how many miles you may have left to go.

Use the space below to jot down some notes about your daily workouts or goals.

SUNDAY   MILES _____

MONDAY   MILES _____

TUESDAY   MILES _____

WEDNESDAY   MILES _____

THURSDAY   MILES _____

FRIDAY   MILES _____

SATURDAY   MILES _____

TOTAL MILES _____

35

UNDER HIS WINGS

He will cover you with his feathers, and under his wings
you will find refuge; his faithfulness will be your shield and
rampart.

Psalm 91:4

FAITH FUEL

One of my favorite things to do when I'm running is to listen and
watch for birds. I have often watched them take a few steps across
the path ahead, then run and begin to flap their wings, eventually
taking flight. It's a beautiful process to watch them uniquely walk,
run, and then soar to new heights.

After an extremely low point in my life, a group of my girlfriends came over to my house and totally redecorated my bed-
room. They painted the furniture, added new light fixtures, re-
arranged the room, and found new art for the walls. They helped
me to transform a place that had been like a hospital room for
several months into a place of peace and refuge.

One of my friends, Bergen, sewed a beautiful blue and white throw pillow for my bed with these words stitched on it: "He will cover you with his feathers, and under his wings you will find refuge" (Psalm 91:4). An embroidered pair of birds are perched on a branch next to the verse. This special pillow has moved with me to two different houses. The pillow bears a message I hold close to my heart, reminding me of God's comfort and faithfulness on my grief journey.

The psalmist uses several images from Psalm 91 to express the ultimate sense of security we find in a relationship with God. The image in verse 4 is of a baby bird covered by its mother's feathers. Bird feathers are known to be a fantastic form of insulation against the cold. This is why many people love down pillows and comforters. Some feathers are coated with oil, which creates a waterproofing effect to protect birds from rain and snow. As the verse says, we can find refuge under His wings. Throughout the Bible are many examples of imagery related to birds, feathers, and wings. In Ruth 2:12, Boaz encourages the young Moabite widow Ruth with these words: "May you be richly rewarded by the LORD, the God of Israel, under whose wings you have come to take refuge." In Psalm 17:8, David writes, "Keep me as the apple of your eye; hide me in the shadow of your wings." Later, in Psalm 57:1, David says, "I will take refuge in the shadow of your wings until the disaster has passed."

These verses emphasize God's character as Protector, Comforter, Shelter, and Strength. When we are hidden in His shadow or under His wings, we are protected like a bird from the elements and from the enemy, who hunts us down. We are not left vulnerable and out in the open, but protected in a safe place.

I've often said running has been my grief therapy after my husband Ericlee's death. When I am out running on the road or a trail, God meets me there. He covers my broken heart with His feathers and provides a safe shelter to share my feelings, my emotions, and my fears. He has been my refuge like He was for David, Ruth, and countless others in the Bible.

The other day I saw a photograph of a mother bird with wings extended like arms around her two birdlings on either side. At a quick glance, the babies looked like they were part of the mama's body because they were enveloped by her feathers. This picture is a perfect visual of what God does for us.

Friend, rest today under His wings. Whether you are walking or running, let Him shelter your heart and provide the strength you need to eventually soar.

FAITH STEP: How has God been a refuge and shelter for you? Can you think of any examples of times when you felt His comfort? Before you start your next run, imagine God covering you in the shadow of His wings. Now is the time to soar!

INSPIRATION: "If you want to become the best runner you can be, start now. Don't spend the rest of your life wondering if you can do it."

   —PRISCILLA WELCH, former British women's marathon record holder

NOTES FROM COACH SHAWN: Progression runs are fantastic workouts; they entail running each successive mile faster than the one before it. If you are slowing down at the end of an easy long run or your interval pace tails off during the last half, it means you started the workout too fast.

Use the space below to jot down some notes about your daily workouts or goals.

SUNDAY   MILES

MONDAY   MILES _____

TUESDAY   MILES _____

WEDNESDAY   MILES _____

THURSDAY   MILES _____

FRIDAY   MILES _____

SATURDAY   MILES _____

TOTAL MILES _____

36

RUNNING TO WORSHIP

So here's what I want you to do, God helping you: Take your
everyday, ordinary life—your sleeping, eating, going-to-work,
and walking-around life—and place it before God as an offering. Embracing what God does for you is the best thing you
can do for him.

Romans 12:1 MSG

FAITH FUEL

One of my favorite running heroes is a man named Eric Liddell
(known as the Flying Scotsman). Eric was a sprinter who inspired
the Oscar-winning movie *Chariots of Fire*. He won the gold medal
in the 400-meter dash during the Paris Olympics in 1924, and he
also went down in history for refusing to run an Olympic race on
a Sunday because of his religious beliefs.

He's famous for this quote: "God made me fast. And when I
run, I feel his pleasure."[1] Eric understood that running was not just
for his personal glory and to win medals; he felt God's pleasure
when he ran because he was doing what God designed him to do.

Romans 12:1 urges us to take our everyday, ordinary life and place it before God as an offering. Eric offered up running to God as his spiritual act of worship. We don't have to go to a church building to experience worship. The English word *worship* means "to ascribe worth to something." Worship is an invitation to commune with our Creator. Worship is a way we can individually and collectively ascribe worth to God and bring Him glory. God invites us to worship in a diversity of ways.

The Message describes it this way: "So here's what I want you to do, God helping you: Take your everyday, ordinary life—your sleeping, eating, going-to-work, and walking-around life—and place it before God as an offering. Embracing what God does for you is the best thing you can do for him" (Romans 12:1). In other words, we can worship God while we sing, cook, wash dishes, drive, work, rest, and yes, even while we run.

Worship has the power to lift our spirits, to turn us toward hope, and to change the landscape of our hearts. When I notice God's glory in the midst of hard days, I can't help but respond in worship. Worship music and running helps lift me from heart-heaviness. It doesn't make sense, but my heart feels lighter when I am out on a trail or when I'm singing. Sometimes I do both.

Running is a physical activity where we can offer up our bodies in worship and experience God. I find myself breathing in His presence as my footsteps lead me on a winding trail through the forest or along a hillside. As I run, there is space for my soul to sing and express my gratitude to God. I see glimpses of His glory in the cheery yellow wildflowers and the billowing clouds in the distance. This is all part of worship.

In 1 Corinthians 10:31, Paul exhorts us, "So, whether you eat or drink, or whatever you do, do all to the glory of God" (ESV). His point was that we can worship God in everything we do to the best of our ability. Eric Liddell adapted this idea in his own life and training: "In the dust of defeat as well as the laurels of victory there is a glory to be found if one has done his best," he said.[2] Whether in his running or his mission work, Eric was always intentional to give the glory back to God. Friend, are you facing some dark circumstance today? Are you traversing a valley? Are you navigating through grief and loss? Run to worship. It can change the landscape of your heart. God will meet you there.

FAITH STEP: What if we had a posture of worship each time we went out to walk and run? What might this look like for you? Are there any songs that help you worship? Take some time to check out the songs on the Walk, Run, Soar playlist on Spotify today, or create your own playlist for running and worship.

INSPIRATION: "To give anything less than your best is to sacrifice the gift."

—STEVE PREFONTAINE, American Olympic distance runner during the 1970s

NOTES FROM COACH SHAWN: Listening to music while running has several benefits. It can energize you, take your mind off of running, and get you in a good rhythm. However, if you're running outside, please be sure you can hear traffic, cyclists, and other runners around you.

Use the space below to jot down some notes about your daily workouts or goals.

SUNDAY   MILES

MONDAY   MILES

TUESDAY	MILES

WEDNESDAY	MILES

THURSDAY	MILES

FRIDAY	MILES

SATURDAY	MILES

TOTAL MILES

37

TRAINING TOGETHER

And let us consider how we may spur one another on toward love and good deeds, not giving up meeting together, as some are in the habit of doing, but encouraging one another—and all the more as you see the Day approaching.

Hebrews 10:24–25

FAITH FUEL

Shawn used to be the co-owner of our local running store. Years ago, he wanted to bring together some of the runners he knew in the community, so he decided to start a running group. In the beginning, fifteen people showed up for this informal time of training together in community.

Eventually, Shawn made this running group into an official nonprofit running club and registered with the Road Runners Clubs of America. Today, the club is called Sierra Challenge Express and boasts more than five hundred members. They run together regularly, put on races, raise money for scholarships, and volunteer in the community.

The spirit of the group is so encouraging. There are talented runners on the team, but the atmosphere is always about community over competition. I'm grateful to train in community, especially on hot days when it would be so much easier to stay at home in the air-conditioning. I find myself working harder because of the inspiration of others running in front of me or by my side.

Coach Ray and Coach Rich challenge all of us with their strategic workouts. They organize the large group into smaller groups at similar skill levels. Coach Ray, who introduces himself as "Old Man Ray," has been coaching the team for more than twenty years and has years of experience as a distance runner himself. He loves to tease and trash-talk the runners just as much as he cheers and challenges us to go farther and faster. He jokes about being too old to race now, but we all know he has earned the street cred to coach us well.

Meanwhile, Coach Rich is the encourager. He calls everyone "baby," and always brings chilled fruit and water to serve at the end of our workouts. He is committed and faithful to the team, and he cultivates community among the members with his gift of encouragement.

In Hebrews, the author encourages believers to have concern for each other and to challenge each other in positive ways. Hebrews 10:24–25 says, "And let us consider how we may *spur one another on* toward love and good deeds, not giving up meeting together, as some are in the habit of doing, but encouraging one another—and all the more as you see the Day approaching." Some translations use different phrases. Instead of "spur one another on," they say, "stir up one another" (NIRV), "stimulate one another" (NASB), or "motivate one another" (NLT). The idea is that we are to move each other forward in the direction of love and good deeds.

When I train with the Sierra Challenge Express team or with other runner friends, I'm more likely to wake up early for my runs because I know someone will be there. There's accountability in knowing the coaches and other teammates will spur me on.

Maybe you've experienced this kind of healthy competition and community that motivates you to train harder than you might on your own. If you haven't, join me in seeking it out. I believe this is what the author of Hebrews was getting at in chapter 10. God designed us as humans to train together.

FAITH STEP: Have you ever been a part of a running or walking group? Is there someone you can connect with this season for accountability and encouragement? Reach out to someone today by text or in person. Share your goals and ask them about theirs.

INSPIRATION: "A goal is just an awesome way to force growth on yourself."

—DEENA KASTOR, American women's marathon record holder

NOTES FROM COACH SHAWN: Joining a local community running club is a wonderful way to meet others with your passion, find training buddies, and learn more about running. Oftentimes they will have group runs, travel to races together, and may even receive discounts to race events. Each running club may have a different emphasis, such as elite racing, trail running, youth participation, or recreational running. Find a club that matches your goals.

Use the space below to jot down some notes about your daily workouts or goals.

SUNDAY   MILES _____

MONDAY   MILES _____

TUESDAY   MILES _____

WEDNESDAY   MILES _____

THURSDAY   MILES _____

FRIDAY   MILES _____

SATURDAY   MILES _____

TOTAL MILES _____

38

FOLLOWING MY COACH

Iron sharpens iron, and one man sharpens another.

Proverbs 27:17 ESV

FAITH FUEL

A cool breeze kissed my cheeks that morning while angled light danced across the trail. Nothing like a long Sunday run to start my Sabbath. I was training for the Shadow of the Giants 20K, so Shawn and I went hunting for "hills for breakfast," as they say. I ran this race before, so I knew what to expect: hills and more hills, and one amazing race through the giant Sequoias. That's why I had to practice running hills beforehand.

Shawn led me for a seven-mile hill training run on the trails and streets of Valencia, California, near his mom's house. There's surprising comfort in letting someone else lead, especially if you have confidence they are following God's guidance. I trust Shawn to know which route to take and how much I can handle. He pushes me in quiet ways to work harder than I might on my own.

I simply fix my eyes on my coach's calves and put one foot in front of the other to follow them.

As we were running those hills, I couldn't help reflecting on how much of my relationship with Shawn has been running up and down hills. He joined my three daughters and me while we were scaling the steep peak of grief. And he has journeyed with us through many hills and valleys these last five years.

We have faced big decisions as a family. Through it all, I appreciate Shawn's steadfastness and gentleness in leading us to discern the voice of God. He is one of the few people in my life who pushes me to dream big and pursue where God is leading me in my career. He is my biggest cheerleader and my hardest editor. He is my prayer warrior and running partner. I am deeply grateful for the chance to grow and bloom with this man as my hubby and coach.

Proverbs 27:17 says, "Iron sharpens iron, and one man sharpens another" (ESV). The imagery here is that when iron is rubbed against iron, it actually sharpens both pieces. Similarly, when two people are running through life together, they can sharpen or challenge each other to new heights. They can keep each other accountable physically and spiritually. They can lift each other up and point each other back to God.

I hear Shawn's simple coaching words: "This hill is steep, but you're almost to the top." I am reminded that we run these hills together to discipline our bodies and prepare our minds for race day. Just these few words from my coach inspire me to lift my knees and breathe deeply to crest that final hill.

Friend, are you facing a hill or series of hills in your life? Our Coach is inviting us to follow His lead. He carried a cross up a hill and died on it so we would never have to run alone. Lift up your eyes. He is coaching you to the top of this hill, and the next, and the next.

FAITH STEP: Have you ever had a coach who made an impact on you? What did he or she do that is memorable? Next time you are running or walking uphill, imagine Jesus running right in front of you. Let Him coach you to the top.

INSPIRATION: "In the midst of an ordinary training day, I try to remind myself that I am preparing for the extraordinary."

—SHALANE FLANAGAN, 2017 New York City Marathon champion

NOTES FROM COACH SHAWN: A coach can help you achieve goals by being a voice of encouragement and also a voice of restraint. A coach should motivate you to challenge your boundaries, but also rein you in when you try to do too much.

Use the space below to jot down some notes about your daily workouts or goals.

SUNDAY   MILES _____

MONDAY   MILES _____

TUESDAY   MILES _____

WEDNESDAY   MILES _____

THURSDAY   MILES _____

FRIDAY   MILES _____

SATURDAY   MILES _____

TOTAL MILES _____

39

RESTING IN UNFORCED RHYTHMS

"Are you tired? Worn out? Burned out on religion? Come to me. Get away with me and you'll recover your life. I'll show you how to take a real rest. Walk with me and work with me—watch how I do it. Learn the unforced rhythms of grace. I won't lay anything heavy or ill-fitting on you. Keep company with me and you'll learn to live freely and lightly."

Matthew 11:28–30 MSG

FAITH FUEL

The other morning I went for a run on the Winchell Cove Trail. It's one of my favorite spots, and I love going there in all different seasons. I was mesmerized anew by the waves of golden grasses undulating over the hills, the cerulean blue of the sky, and the branches of the trees stretching in a dance toward heaven. Water lapped at the shore below. My trail shoes connected with the earth, tracing the sapphire edges of Millerton Lake.

I know it sounds counterintuitive, but trail running has taught me to rest. Some people think running is *not* resting. To me, there's something inspiring about running free on a winding trail with God's glory unfolding all around me. When I'm running, my heart stills and leans in to hear God speak.

I have discovered, as a forty-year-old mama of three active daughters, that rest in my daily life looks a little different than I expected. I have shifted my thinking about rest. It's not always about pedicures, weekends away, and sleeping in. I know that by nature I am a highly motivated, multitasking mama. I have to be intentional to carve out time and give myself permission for what I call "soul care."

This kind of rest requires saying "no" to constant striving, mindless scrolling, friend comparison, unbridled fear, and sticky guilt. A real rest for our souls is about running to God for all our needs. It's paying attention to our minds, bodies, and souls.

The world tells us we are entitled to self-care. The trouble with this is the methods are often scripted and expensive. Rest and soul care don't need to cost a lot of money, but it does require time. It involves turning down the noise in our worlds and entering into His presence in a personal way.

I love Eugene Peterson's version of Matthew 11:28–30. *The Message* says, "Are you tired? Worn out? Burned out on religion? Come to me. Get away with me and you'll recover your life. I'll show you how to take a real rest. Walk with me and work with me—watch how I do it. Learn the unforced rhythms of grace. I won't lay anything heavy or ill-fitting on you. Keep company with me and you'll learn to live freely and lightly."

These verses express God's desire for us to "come," "get away," "walk with," and "keep company" with Him. He desires "real rest" for us, not the rest that makes you feel like you need a vacation from your vacation when you return home. He provides a more in-depth, restorative rest when we spend time with Him. When I'm out on the trail, I find rest by basking in the glory of His creation. I make running time prayer-conversation time with Him.

I want to challenge you with this question: Where can your heart be still and rest in God?

God is calling each one of us to regular rhythms of rest. This might look different for you than it does for me. You will need to work it out with your attitude, your schedule, and your family context. The goal is to find out what engages your soul. We are invited to seek the Savior daily and discover unforced rhythms of rest. Rest is a gift from a good Father who longs to see all of us flourish.

FAITH STEP: I encourage you to try a new practice. Take a walk at a nearby park. Jog in a different direction than you normally go. Choose a trail run to go in search of His glory. Make your walk or run into a time for noticing, listening, and praying. See what God reveals to you when you work with Him.

INSPIRATION: "During the hard training phase, never be afraid to take a day off. If your legs are feeling unduly stiff and sore, rest; if you are at all sluggish, rest; in fact, if in doubt, rest."

—BRUCE FORDYCE, South African ultramarathoner

NOTES FROM COACH SHAWN: Regularly schedule rest and recovery phases throughout your training schedule for complete physical, mental, and emotional rejuvenation.

Use the space below to jot down some notes about your daily workouts or goals.

SUNDAY   MILES _____

MONDAY   MILES _____

TUESDAY   MILES _____

WEDNESDAY   MILES _____

THURSDAY   MILES _____

FRIDAY   MILES _____

SATURDAY   MILES _____

TOTAL MILES _____

40

RUNNING TOWARD THE ROCK

He only is my rock and my salvation, my fortress; I shall not be shaken. On God rests my salvation and my glory; my mighty rock, my refuge is God.

Psalm 62:6–7 ESV

FAITH FUEL

The ocean has always been my happy place. Ever since I was a little girl, I have found refuge near the water's edge. There's something about the crash of the waves, the salty air tickling my tongue, and the breathtaking sunsets that calm my soul and inspire me all at once.

I have run over a diversity of terrains these last few years, but recently I experienced my first time running an actual race on the beach. I participated in the Rock'n Around the Pier Half Marathon from Morro Rock to Cayucos Pier in California. This out-and-back trail run was quite literally on the hard-packed sand along the Pacific Ocean. This memorial run was started to honor runner and teacher Brian Waterbury, who died of melanoma cancer in 2003, a cancer with which our family was all too familiar.

We rode a charter bus with about thirty-five friends from our Sierra Challenge Express running club. When we disembarked the bus, we were greeted by the misty, cool air of the central coast. This was a welcome contrast to the temperatures that soared in the triple digits in the central valley, where we live. Fog seeped over the hills and spilled out over the ocean, creating an ethereal atmosphere at the start of this race.

I generally run with my earbuds pumping a carefully curated playlist of music, but there was no need for music when all creation was singing to me. The waves, the wind, the birds. We weaved through kelp, crunched over sand dollars, avoided crabs, and leapt over rivulets of water.

I ran more than ten miles, but then my feet hit soft sand. I was running but getting nowhere fast. My chest burned. The salty air stung my eyes. The journey had suddenly become much harder than I anticipated, and my body was not prepared.

I felt like Moses and the Israelites standing in the darkness before the Red Sea: "The LORD drove the sea back by a strong east wind and turned it into dry land. The waters were divided" (Exodus 14:21). God was working through my darkness to hold back this sea of grief. If He could harness the wind and these ocean waves, He could surely help me navigate any rough waters.

Eyes still stinging, I saw Shawn. He had finished the race and returned, looking for me. I felt hope rising. I found the rhythm of my feet hitting hard sand again. I strained and squinted for that arch that marked the finish. Shawn kept telling me it was there, but I couldn't make out the black letters through the mist. All I could see was the Great Rock—Morro Rock—rising glorious and majestic before me.

I ran toward it. The words of the psalmist were suddenly on my lips: "My rock and my salvation, my fortress; I shall not be shaken. On God rests my salvation and my glory; my mighty rock, my refuge is God" (Psalm 62:6–7 ESV).

Do you feel like you are drowning in waves of grief or struggle or pain? Are you squinting through the mist for that elusive finish line? Are your feet slipping as you run through the soft sand? Friend, I encourage you to run toward the Rock. The waves of grief will come and go, ebb and flow, but the Rock will provide a steady refuge.

FAITH STEP: Have you experienced grief or loss in your life? Briefly describe a few of those losses that have made the biggest impact on you. How has God been a rock for you in difficult times? While you run, meditate on these words from Psalm 62: "My rock and my salvation, my fortress; I shall not be shaken."

INSPIRATION: "When I am running, I run with no fear. I try to perform like that. If somebody even follows me, I don't have fear."

—GEOFFREY MUTAI, 2011 Boston Marathon and New York Marathon champion

NOTES FROM COACH SHAWN: It's common to be nervous leading into a race, wondering if you trained properly, if your race day nutrition plan will work, or if you are wearing the right shoes. Cast out those fears by reflecting back on all the hard workouts you completed to boost your confidence and focus on the race one mile at a time.

Use the space below to jot down some notes about your daily workouts or goals.

SUNDAY   MILES _____

MONDAY   MILES _____

TUESDAY   MILES _____

WEDNESDAY   MILES _____

THURSDAY   MILES _____

FRIDAY   MILES _____

SATURDAY   MILES _____

TOTAL MILES _____

41

DEVELOPING
MENTAL TOUGHNESS

We use our powerful God-tools for smashing warped philosophies, tearing down barriers erected against the truth of God,
fitting every loose thought and emotion and impulse into the
structure of life shaped by Christ.

2 Corinthians 10:5 MSG

FAITH FUEL

I always love an adventure, especially if it involves a new trail and
a group of girlfriends. We truly didn't know what to expect when
we signed up to run the Tar Springs Ranch trail run. The pictures
looked beautiful, and who could resist a road trip to California's
central coast? We booked a little Airbnb near Pismo Beach, and
six of us started training.

We knew it was a hilly course, but none of us were quite ready
for the hills upon muddy hills we would face on race day. When
the race started, the mist was thick and I was shoulder-to-shoulder

with my friend Marina. We ran through a grove of oak trees with branches that swayed like arms dancing. Lush green foliage carpeted the forest. The tangy-sweet smell of wet bark and earth wafted to my nose. I felt like we were running through a scene from one of the *Lord of the Rings* movies.

The rocky path curved and pointed us upward. The mist turned into fog, which clouded our view of what was ahead. We tackled one hill at a time. Eventually, we had to embrace the rain that dripped from every flower petal and fern and soaked our clothes.

These hills were steep. And just when we made it to the top of one, another would appear. I knew I had to tap in to some mental toughness if I was going to make it through this race. Running coaches often talk about the importance of mental toughness. They encourage athletes to cultivate mental toughness by training hard and pushing beyond what they believe they can do.

Mental toughness is a psychology term, referring to resilience and strength that helps us soldier through struggles and succeed. Mental toughness is key for athletes, equipping them to remain strong, confident, and competitive. It gives us the ability to push past exhaustion, obstacles, and even injuries.

The apostle Paul wrote two letters to the church he planted in Corinth, addressing the persistent problems of the church. In 2 Corinthians, he is concerned about the false apostles who have been trying to shake the faith of the Christians in Corinth.

He writes, "We use our powerful God-tools for smashing warped philosophies, tearing down barriers erected against the truth of God, fitting every loose thought and emotion and impulse into the structure of life shaped by Christ" (2 Corinthians 10:5 MSG). In other words, he's encouraging them and us to be ready for battle. We need to be mentally tough and grounded in the truth we know about Christ and the gospel.

In life and running, negative thoughts and lies will creep in when we least expect them. We have to throw those thoughts in jail. When I was running at Tar Springs Ranch, I had to push past my tiredness on those steep hills. In fact, I couldn't even allow the word *tired* to linger in my mind. I had to throw that word in jail and replace it with words like *lift*, *push*, and *soar*. When we are obedient to Christ, He helps us to the finish line.

During the Tar Springs Ranch race, we climbed a total of 1,488 feet. When the finish was in sight, I started to sprint. My friend Marina looked at me and said, "Go!" She was setting me free to fly to the finish. I found one more gear deep inside me and kicked it up a notch. Although we all finished at different times, all six of us mamas completed the race and celebrated in the rain with tacos and root beer.

FAITH STEP: What is one area where you need to develop mental toughness in your life today? Identify a few negative words or phrases that run through your mind when you are tired or discouraged. Write them down. Then cross these words out and replace them with a few words that might uplift you when the race gets hard or the hill is steep before you. Practice reciting these words in your mind the next time you run or walk.

INSPIRATION: "I go beyond what I think is possible; I punish myself and really learn to suffer. That gives me the peace of mind and confidence to know that when I'm racing and it hurts, I can overcome it. When I get off the bike, for instance, I don't think: 'Oh Lordy, I've got a marathon to do.' I think, 'Bring it on.'"

—CHRISSIE WELLINGTON, four-time Ironman world champion

NOTES FROM COACH SHAWN: In a race, spend time monitoring the signals your body is sending you. Where are you tight, how is your breathing, where are you chafing, and where are you hurting? Make small adjustments in your stride or pace to alleviate any hindrances.

Use the space below to jot down some notes about your daily workouts or goals.

SUNDAY   MILES _____

MONDAY   MILES _____

TUESDAY   MILES _____

WEDNESDAY   MILES _____

THURSDAY   MILES _____

FRIDAY   MILES _____

SATURDAY   MILES _____

TOTAL MILES _____

42

BUILDING MUSCLE MEMORY

So I run with purpose in every step. I am not just shadowboxing. I discipline my body like an athlete, training it to do what it
should. Otherwise, I fear that after preaching to others I myself
might be disqualified.

1 Corinthians 9:26–27 NLT

FAITH FUEL

Sometimes life happens. We are forced to take a break from training and running. This might be necessitated by an injury, a vacation, a holiday, or simply a too-busy season. The good news is
that the time we have invested in running in the past can help us
in the future.

They call it muscle memory. By definition, muscle memory is
the ability to reproduce a particular movement without conscious
thought. Muscle memory comes when there is frequent repetition
of a movement. Our muscles don't literally have memories, but our
brains do remember what it feels like to exercise in a certain way.

Meanwhile, when we strengthen our muscles, they generate more nuclei, or "little protein factories," that contain DNA necessary for increasing muscle volume. Even if we take a break from running, those nuclei stick around, which helps us get back into running more quickly in the future if we take a break.

In running, it's critical to practice proper form, pacing, and breathing so our bodies and brains remember what to do when we get out on the road or trail. When Shawn builds training programs, he has his runners start out with lower miles and increase to longer distances over time. That way the body gets used to running and pushing a little farther each time. On race day, 13.1 miles feels less overwhelming to the body if the person has already run twelve miles in training. There's muscle memory.

When we coach our track-and-field and cross-country teams, we teach the kids warm-up drills that we repeat every time we practice. Some of these drills include marching with straight legs kicking out, running with knees lifted high, skipping, running while bending at the knees and kicking your rear, and more. The main idea is to pay attention and make meaningful movements. These drills help train the brain and muscles so when the kids are running, jumping, or throwing in their various track-and-field events, their bodies know what to do.

This concept of muscle memory can carry over to our spiritual lives. When we purposefully engage in spiritual disciplines, it's like creating muscle memory in our souls. Our souls begin to form spiritual habits when we do the things Jesus did. He studied, prayed, fasted, confessed, worshiped, rested, celebrated, served, and gave generously. I've found in my own life that some of these practices have helped me walk through the challenging seasons. I return to prayer, Scripture, and naming God's gifts to me as a place of refuge.

In 1 Corinthians 9, Paul talks about purpose. He explains that his primary purpose in life is to spread the Good News and share in its blessings. Then he makes an analogy to the athletic life and running. He writes, "Don't you realize that in a race everyone runs, but only one person gets the prize? So run to win! All athletes are disciplined in their training. They do it to win a prize that will fade away, but we do it for an eternal prize. So I run with purpose in every step. I am not just shadowboxing. I discipline my body like an athlete, training it to do what it should. Otherwise, I fear that after preaching to others I myself might be disqualified" (1 Corinthians 9:24–27 NLT).

The key here is that Paul is exhorting us to "run with purpose in every step." We have to "run to win," which means training well and giving it our best effort. We can't just preach the Good News to others; you and I have to discipline ourselves like athletes so we can live out the Good News and make it to the finish line.

FAITH STEP: Jesus studied, prayed, fasted, confessed, worshiped, rested, celebrated, served, and gave generously. Choose one of these spiritual disciplines you'd like to work on in your own life. Write out a few ideas of how you can be committed to this practice in the upcoming month.

INSPIRATION: "When a person trains once, nothing happens. When a person forces himself to do a thing a hundred or a thousand times, then he certainly has developed in more ways than physical. Is it raining? That doesn't matter. Am I tired? That doesn't matter either. If one can stick to the training throughout the many long years, then willpower is no longer a problem."

—EMIL ZÁTOPEK, Czechoslovakian distance runner who won three gold medals at the 1952 Olympics

NOTES FROM COACH SHAWN: Consistent running over several years is the key to building running endurance and strength. It takes years of running and mileage to maximize your strength and aerobic conditioning. Think long-term if you want to race at your best in the marathon.

Use the space below to jot down some notes about your daily workouts or goals.

SUNDAY   MILES _____

MONDAY   MILES _____

TUESDAY   MILES _____

WEDNESDAY   MILES _____

THURSDAY   MILES _____

FRIDAY   MILES _____

SATURDAY   MILES _____

TOTAL MILES _____

43

RUN LIKE A GIRL

"And now, go quickly and tell his disciples that he has risen from the dead, and he is going ahead of you to Galilee. You will see him there. Remember what I have told you." The women ran quickly from the tomb. They were very frightened but also filled with great joy, and they rushed to give the disciples the angel's message.

Matthew 28:7–8 NLT

FAITH FUEL

I have coached a sweet girl named Hannah from elementary school and now into junior high. When I first met Hannah at cross-country practice, I saw she had raw talent. She was also very unsure of herself and her abilities. Through that first season, Hannah got a taste of what it's like to train and compete. She was a hard worker, but she was often hard on herself and ended up in tears after races. We spent a lot of time running together and working through those emotions.

Hannah has a shirt she often wears that says, "I run like a girl," and on the back it says, "Try to keep up." Every time she wears that shirt, I can't help but smile inside. The shirt serves as a reminder of how far she's come.

Over the last five years, I have watched Hannah grow and mature. Somewhere along the way, she found her wings. Her blond ponytail swings behind her, and her slender legs run with confidence now. You can see the joy on her face as she flies around the track.

In the Bible we read stories of several women who lacked confidence at first, but whom Jesus healed and used in important ways throughout His ministry. The women who followed Jesus from Galilee and ministered with Him were there when His body was brought to the tomb after He died on the cross. Mary Magdalene (whom Jesus delivered from seven demons), the other Mary (mother of James), Salome (mother of James and John), and Joanna (wife of Chuza, Herod's steward) brought spices to the tomb on the day after the Sabbath (Matthew 28; Luke 24:10). There was a great earthquake, and an angel as bright as lightning and dressed in white descended from heaven. The guards were quaking in their sandals.

The angel spoke purposefully to the women: "Don't be afraid!" he said. "I know you are looking for Jesus, who was crucified. He isn't here! He is risen from the dead, just as he said would happen. Come, see where his body was lying. And now, go quickly and tell his disciples that he has risen from the dead, and he is going ahead of you to Galilee. You will see him there. Remember what I have told you" (Matthew 28:5–7 NLT).

The angel chose to share this message about Jesus' resurrection with the women first. There are myriad other more grandiose ways He could have announced this, but God chose to use an angel to reach out personally to the women whose lives were transformed by His Son. He invited them to be the first eyewitnesses, the messengers, the carriers of this Good News.

The women wasted no time. They ran. I imagine them picking up their skirts in their hands and running with all their strength. These girls were fueled by joy and wild wonder. The only one who could keep up with them was Jesus himself. He stops them in their tracks. "And as they went, Jesus met them and greeted them. And they ran to him, grasped his feet, and worshiped him. Then Jesus said to them, 'Don't be afraid! Go tell my brothers to leave for Galilee, and they will see me there'" (Matthew 28:9–10 NLT).

These women were given the awesome privilege of testifying that Jesus had risen from the dead just as He said He would. In their culture, it might have been difficult to convince the disciples and others this was true because Jewish men did not consider women to be reliable witnesses, but Jesus reassures them not to be afraid. Like the angel, He urges them to go and tell the brothers He is coming.

I had the privilege of helping train my friend Hannah to run her first half marathon last year. Not many twelve-year-olds are signing up to run 13.1 miles with their coach. That girl pushed the pace as we ran the first seven miles together. Then I set her free to fly to the finish on her own. Like Mary Magdalene and the other women Jesus met after His resurrection, she was not afraid to run like a girl.

FAITH STEP: Have you ever lacked confidence? Can you recall someone or something that helped you gain courage to keep running your race? Who can you encourage in a similar way today? Take a moment to text or call a friend to impart courage like Jesus did.

INSPIRATION: "Life is for participating, not for spectating."

—KATHRINE SWITZER, first woman to officially enter the Boston Marathon

NOTES FROM COACH SHAWN: Keep a journal about your running experiences. Capture your feelings and thoughts about your training, highlight your favorite runs, and describe any other reflections. These writings will be priceless memories to relive someday and provide inspiration to continue running.

Use the space below to jot down some notes about your daily workouts or goals.

SUNDAY   MILES _____

MONDAY   MILES _____

TUESDAY   MILES _____

WEDNESDAY   MILES _____

THURSDAY   MILES _____

FRIDAY   MILES _____

SATURDAY   MILES _____

TOTAL MILES _____

44

LEARNING FROM THE CREPE MYRTLE

"Instead of the thorn shall come up the cypress; instead of the brier shall come up the myrtle; and it shall make a name for the Lord, an everlasting sign that shall not be cut off."

Isaiah 55:13 ESV

FAITH FUEL

This morning I went "glory chasing" with my friend Stephanie. When we run together, we hunt for pictures of God's glory in creation. We talk about the evidence of God working in our lives. We encourage each other to chase God's glory in both the mundane and life's challenges.

On this particular day, we ran on the cow loop trail at the base of Woodward Park. We paused several times to marvel at God's creation. Little frogs jumped on spindly legs through the grasses, bunnies bobbed across the trail, birds danced on the wire fences, the sun promenaded in brilliant colors over the hills—all these singing of His glory. This must have been what David meant in the Psalms when he wrote, "The heavens declare the glory of God, and the sky above proclaims his handiwork" (Psalm 19:1 ESV).

We tried to take pictures, but none of them quite captured the true beauty of what we saw. Taking time to behold these precious glimpses of God's glory lifted my spirits from my own challenges. His creation reminded me that He is God. He is creative, sovereign, and full of glory. He invites each of us to experience His glory and peace through the intricacies of nature.

But it was the crepe myrtle near the end of our run that made me stop in my tracks. Her branches were dressed in white flowers like a vintage lace wedding gown. She stood so regal at the end of the path, and yet somehow whispered kindness and grace over me as I ran on tired, sore legs.

Sometimes nature teaches us the most profound lessons. Stephanie told me about the beautiful pink crepe myrtles planted in her own neighborhood. The crepe myrtle is a hearty plant known for her long blooming season. She can withstand the heat—even the triple-digit temperatures of Fresno where we live—although she prefers shade.

The prophet Isaiah talks about the myrtle as a symbol of life and abundance: "Instead of the thorn shall come up the cypress; instead of the brier shall come up the myrtle; and it shall make a name for the LORD, an everlasting sign that shall not be cut off" (Isaiah 55:13 ESV). The myrtle is contrasted to the brier. She is resilient, robust, and flourishing.

I found myself saying a little prayer in my head while we finished our run: *God, make me like the crepe myrtle. Help me enjoy the details of today whether in heat or shade. Allow me to be a sweet fragrance, reflecting your glory to others. Amen.*

And this is what it means to be a "glory chaser," my friends. It's having eyes to look up and see God's handiwork even when the heat and the hills of life's trails tempt us to focus too much on our own burning feet. It's receiving His lavish love for us each day and pointing others to His glory like the crepe myrtle.

FAITH STEP: How have you experienced God's glory through creation? No matter what you are going through today, take some time to notice the beauty around you. Slow down and savor. Write down in detail three things you saw on your run that displayed God's glory.

INSPIRATION: "Set aside time solely for running. Running is more fun if you don't have to rush through it."

—JIM FIXX, author of *The Complete Book of Running*

NOTES FROM COACH SHAWN: Wear a hat or visor to protect your head, prevent sweat from dripping into your eyes, and shade your face. This will protect your face from the harsh sun and minimize squinting, which can tense up your head, neck, and shoulders.

Use the space below to jot down some notes about your daily workouts or goals.

SUNDAY   MILES

MONDAY   MILES

TUESDAY   MILES

WEDNESDAY   MILES _____

THURSDAY   MILES _____

FRIDAY   MILES _____

SATURDAY   MILES _____

TOTAL MILES _____

45

RUNNING AGAINST
THE WIND

Later that night, the boat was in the middle of the lake, and he
was alone on land. He saw the disciples straining at the oars,
because the wind was against them.

Mark 6:47–48

FAITH FUEL

When I signed up to run the Sombrero Half Marathon in Simi
Valley, I had no idea what I would face on race day. This race was
a great excuse to visit Grandma, who lives not too far away, and
run in a new city. Not to mention they gave out sombreros and
served street tacos at the finish line!

We arrived at the start early that Sunday morning since there
wasn't as much traffic as we expected. Our first indication that
this was going to be a windy day was when we saw a Porta Potty
careen across the parking lot. (I shot a prayer of thanks to God
that I was not sitting in that Porta Potty at the time.)

Shawn and our three daughters cheered me on as the race commenced. As promised, the course was very flat with just a few rollers. A few miles in, I realized two reasons why this race would prove challenging. First, there were very few runners, so I was mostly running alone. Second, those Santa Ana winds are strong!

The wind whipped my ponytail wildly. I was forced to squint to keep dust from flying into my eyes. I felt like I was working hard, but I wasn't making a lot of progress—kind of like running on a treadmill with a huge fan blowing in my face. Thankfully, I had my phone. I called Shawn and asked if he could grab my sunglasses and ChapStick to pass them off at the next spot where he planned to meet me. I was desperate for some reprieve.

I remembered the disciples in Matthew 8, who found themselves in a boat in the middle of a storm. The wind whipped against them, and waves started to spill over the side of the boat. Meanwhile, Jesus was napping. The disciples woke Him up. Matthew described it this way: "The disciples went and woke him up, shouting, 'Lord, save us! We're going to drown!' Jesus responded, 'Why are you afraid? You have so little faith!'

Then he got up and rebuked the wind and waves, and suddenly there was a great calm" (Matthew 8:25–26 NLT). These men had been ministering with Jesus. They witnessed Him performing many miracles, but when this storm came, they relied on their own strength and panicked.

In this scene, Jesus demonstrated His power over nature, including the wind and the waves. "The disciples were amazed. 'Who is this man?' they asked. 'Even the winds and waves obey him!'" (Matthew 8:27 NLT). Let's not forget who created the wind and the waves. Jesus worked in tandem with His Father and the Holy Spirit back in Genesis to create all the earth and the elements. They created the wind and had the power to calm it when they chose.

The wind often feels like the trials we face in this life or the pushback we feel when we are following Jesus. Maybe you are like me—too often relying on your own strength to weather the storms. The enemy uses this opportunity to make us feel isolated, alone, and helpless. He would rather we forget about the strength we have in Jesus.

Exodus 14:14 reminds us, "The Lord will fight for you; you need only to be still." Our job is to trust God even when the wind is blowing us back on the trail. Isaiah 54:17 affirms us: "No weapon forged against you will prevail, and you will refute every tongue that accuses you." Friend, we have to cling to these truths and remember Jesus is always in the boat with us. Sometimes He calms the storm and holds back the fierce winds; other times He helps us run through them.

Around mile eleven I saw a woman ahead of me on the path running along the canal in Simi Valley. I decided to follow her so I was not facing the wind alone. I fixed my eyes on her feet and kept running. Before I knew it, we were crossing the finish line. My husband and kids were waiting there with open arms to congratulate me. They placed a sombrero on my head and a medal around my neck. The wind still swirled around us, but I felt surprisingly strong because I knew I was not alone.

FAITH STEP: Can you think of a time when you felt like you were running against the wind? Maybe you experienced this in a race or in one of life's trials. How did you get through the wind? What strategy would you offer someone else who might be feeling push-back or struggling today?

INSPIRATION: "I always loved running. . . . It was something you could do by yourself and under your own power. You could go in any direction, fast or slow as you wanted, fighting the wind if you felt like it, seeking out new sights just on the strength of your feet and the courage of your lungs."

—JESSE OWENS, four-time gold medalist in track-and-field at the 1936 Olympics

NOTES FROM COACH SHAWN: As the temperatures dip, a windbreaker vest or jacket will keep the chill off your chest and block the wind from cutting through you. Also, start a run slower than normal to give your muscles and lungs extra time to warm up. Have a dry set of clothes readily available after a run in cold weather. This will help you cool down at a controlled pace.

Use the space below to jot down some notes about your daily workouts or goals.

SUNDAY   MILES _____

MONDAY   MILES _____

TUESDAY   MILES _____

WEDNESDAY   MILES _____

THURSDAY   MILES _____

FRIDAY   MILES _____

SATURDAY   MILES _____

TOTAL MILES _____

46

FIGHTING THE GOOD FIGHT

I have fought the good fight, I have finished the race, I have
kept the faith.

2 Timothy 4:7

FAITH FUEL

It is never an easy assignment when someone is tasked with choosing what to have engraved on a loved one's headstone after their death. My mother-in-law and I spent some time deciding what my first husband Ericlee's headstone should communicate. We settled on including his name, his birth date and death date with a cross between, and the poignant words of 2 Timothy 4:7: "I have fought the good fight, I have finished the race, I have kept the faith." In so many ways, Ericlee embodied this final charge that Paul gives to his mentee, Timothy.

The apostle Paul declares in his letter to Timothy, "I have fought the good fight." In other words, Paul remained a faithful soldier to God and a defender of the gospel message, despite opposition and persecution. Paul urged Timothy, whom he regarded as a co-laborer and son, to keep on fighting in the same manner.

Paul had to battle for his life and ministry. His second letter to the Corinthian church reveals some of what he experienced in his lifetime. He was imprisoned, flogged, beaten with rods, stoned, shipwrecked, chased by bandits, criticized, hungry, and homeless at different points in his ministry (2 Corinthians 11:23–28).

Paul goes on to write: "I have finished the race." He likens life to a race. This running imagery is peppered throughout his letters. Paul is a disciplined athlete who has trained his body for the course of the Christian life. This statement suggests that Paul is expecting to die soon. He is preparing his protégé, Timothy, for that possibility, while encouraging Timothy to keep his eyes on the finish line and the heavenly prize.

Paul concludes, "I have kept the faith." Paul has been a good steward of what God has entrusted to him. He stays faithful to the truth—never embracing false teaching or veering off from his call to carry the gospel to the Jews and Gentiles.

Paul was a man who ran toward God and godliness. This section of his letter to Timothy is like his "final instructions." He's ready to pass the baton. Paul fixes his eyes on the future: "Now there is in store for me the crown of righteousness, which the Lord, the righteous Judge, will award to me on that day—and not only to me, but also to all who have longed for his appearing" (2 Timothy 4:8). Paul is sprinting down the lane the way the athletes did in the Greek games. The winners were awarded a laurel crown. Paul anticipates an eternal crown of righteousness awarded to all those who finish well in the race called life.

Our world and culture so often emphasize living in the present rather than looking to the eternal.

Many believe Jesus was thirty-three when he died. Scholars say Paul died in his sixties. We simply do not know how long or short our races will be. Each life is like a tiny blip on the timeline of eternity.

Friend, in light of all of this, I urge you to fight the good fight, to run your best race today, and to live the faith with passion until you cross that final finish line!

FAITH STEP: What does it mean to you to "fight the good fight"? In what areas are you fighting right now? What would it look like for you to level up? Write down a few areas you would like to work on so you can run your best life race.

INSPIRATION: "The will to win means nothing without the will to prepare."

—JUMA IKANGAA, 1989 New York City Marathon champion

NOTES FROM COACH SHAWN: Whether it's a long run or intervals on the track, finish faster than you started. This teaches your body to be fast even when it's fatigued.

Use the space below to jot down some notes about your daily workouts or goals.

SUNDAY   MILES _____

MONDAY   MILES _____

TUESDAY   MILES _____

WEDNESDAY   MILES _____

THURSDAY   MILES _____

FRIDAY   MILES _____

SATURDAY   MILES _____

TOTAL MILES _____

47

PRAYING WHILE RUNNING

And pray in the Spirit on all occasions with all kinds of prayers and requests. With this in mind, be alert and always keep on praying for all the Lord's people.

Ephesians 6:18

FAITH FUEL

How do you find time for prayer? I'm discovering in this season of my life that I need to create intentional rhythms of prayer in my life. Often when I wake in the morning, I reach for my phone to turn on worship music, but thirty minutes later I'm still attending to all the alerts and notifications that have collected overnight, and I've completely forgotten about worship and prayer. That's why I'm forcing myself into running shoes and stepping out into morning's light to find quiet.

There's something about running—putting one foot in front of the other at any speed—that helps me focus and quiet my heart. I find myself thanking God for the blooming hibiscus outside my door and pouring out all my burdens. The names of friends and family light up my mind, and I whisper fervent prayers for strength, discernment, and grace. I don't do it every day, but I'm giving myself permission to go out on what I call "prayer runs."

In Ephesians 6:18, Paul reminds us, "And pray in the Spirit on all occasions with all kinds of prayers and requests. With this in mind, be alert and always keep on praying for all the Lord's people." Paul underscores the importance of practicing prayer in all different ways at all different times. Given how much Paul refers to running in his letters, I imagine he would have encouraged prayer runs.

I went on a lot of prayer runs after my first husband's death. While running, I wrestled with God. Hundreds of people across the globe had prayed for months for my husband's healing, and it hadn't come. *Why continue to pray when our prayers weren't answered?*

As a new widow, I struggled to know how to proceed. My faith was strong but my heart felt fragile. My prayers were like desperate whispers released to the heavens as I put one foot in front of the other.

God was patient with me. If He could handle the bold prayers of Paul, the emotional prayers of David, and the heart cries of Job, then He could handle my doubting, imperfect, raw prayers.

Over time, I was reminded that just because we pray doesn't mean we get our way. We don't put in a certain amount of time on the prayer time clock to gain a certain outcome. In fact, the purpose of prayer is not to persuade God to do things our way; it's to draw close to the heavenly Father and abide in His presence.

My heart shifted over time as I realized the purpose of prayer is to connect more intimately with the Father and trust His sovereignty. In my grief, He was close to me. He wept with me. He offered comfort when the ache was heavy and the future seemed hopeless. Now I embrace the sweetness of knowing I can surrender the outcome of every single prayer to a capable and all-knowing God.

While running, He renews our minds and hearts. We can mentally prepare for the day and tasks ahead. We can petition God on behalf of others. We can release our stress and invite Him to replace it with a "peace that passes understanding." In busy seasons, we may have to be more intentional to take time to care for our souls in ways that are restorative. It's not just "me time"; it's "God time" that we really need to feel more whole. I challenge you to make at least one of your runs each week into a prayer run.

Romans 12:2 reminds us, "Do not be conformed to this world, but be transformed by the renewal of your mind, that by testing you may discern what is the will of God, what is good and acceptable and perfect" (ESV).

If I hadn't gotten myself out of bed this morning to run, I know I wouldn't have experienced such a sweet time of connecting with the Father. He showed me this gift at the end of my run: two flowers with petals gently enfolded in each other like the loving embrace of my heavenly Father.

FAITH STEP: Write down ten things you are thankful for today. Maybe it's the sunrise colors waltzing across the sky, or the giggle of your new grandchild, or running without pain, or even connecting with a friend over coffee. Name these little gifts and offer them up to our heavenly Father as a prayer today while you run. Make it a gratitude mile.

INSPIRATION: "Some sessions are stars and some are stones, but in the end they are all rocks and we build upon them."
—CHRISSIE WELLINGTON, four-time Ironman world champion

NOTES FROM COACH SHAWN: Giving a high effort level is one component of running faster, but not at the expense of being relaxed. Simply trying harder will often lead to gritting your teeth, tightening your shoulders, and running with inefficient form. Stay relaxed and fluid as you pick up the pace by mentally monitoring from head to toes the signals your body is sending you. Take a controlled deep breath and exhale to relax any tight area you identify. Train smarter, not harder.

Use the space below to jot down some notes about your daily workouts or goals.

SUNDAY   MILES

MONDAY   MILES

TUESDAY   MILES

WEDNESDAY   MILES

THURSDAY   MILES

FRIDAY   MILES

SATURDAY   MILES

TOTAL MILES

48

NAVIGATING INJURIES

Lord, I wait for you; you will answer, Lord my God.

Psalm 38:15

FAITH FUEL

I've been battling a back injury for the last two weeks. It's a sharp pain in my lower back that sometimes travels down to my right glute. This is the first time I've run in sixteen days. Needless to say, it has been hard and humbling.

I like to think I have a high threshold for pain after running three marathons and over twenty-five half marathons, and having three natural childbirths, but back pain is no joke. I've been icing, stretching, applying essential oils, and basically taking ibuprofen around the clock. It's been rough to sleep and even rougher to sit at my desk or ride in a car.

Today I was able to run two miles. I felt like the Tin Man in *The Wizard of Oz*—creaky and stiff but persevering. I've grown a renewed compassion for my friends who face long-term injuries and chronic pain. I know it's hard to stay mentally in the game and hopeful when your body is screaming.

We all experience some kind of pain in our lifetime. Thankfully, none of us is alone in our pain. In Psalm 38, David writes a lament about his battle with both physical and psychological pain: "My back is filled with searing pain; there is no health in my body. I am feeble and utterly crushed; I groan in anguish of heart. All my longings lie open before you, Lord; my sighing is not hidden from you" (vv. 7–9).

This psalm is full of raw, honest words from a hurting David. What strikes me is David's response from the place of pain: He waits on God; he trusts God to carry him through. In Psalm 38:15, we see evidence of this when he writes, "LORD, I wait for you; you will answer, Lord my God." Several translations use the phrase "I put my hope in you" to give us further understanding of David's posture. He is hurting, discouraged, and burdened, but he still pivots to hope in God.

Throughout the Bible are reminders that God stands with us in our pain. Exodus 14:14 encourages us, "The LORD will fight for you; you need only to be still."

Jeremiah 29:11 reassures us, "'For I know the plans I have for you,' declares the LORD, 'plans to prosper you and not to harm you, plans to give you hope and a future.'"

First Peter 4:1 reminds us that Jesus can relate to pain and suffering: "Therefore, since Christ suffered in his body, arm yourselves also with the same attitude, because whoever suffers in the body is done with sin."

Second Corinthians 4:17 provides comfort and hope: "For light momentary affliction is preparing for us an eternal weight of glory beyond all comparison."

Pain and suffering can serve as important tools in our lives. When we experience pain—whether physical or emotional—we have a choice to turn toward despair or to turn toward hope, as David did. Maybe you're struggling with plantar fasciitis today, or you feel the effects of shin splints. Maybe you have knee or back pain, IT band problems, or some other running injury. Maybe you are facing depression or anxiety. Be patient with yourself and your body, friend. Let the power be in your response to the pain. I'm praying courage, faith, and trust for you today.

FAITH STEP: Are you injured or in pain today? Look up another Bible verse that serves as a reminder of how God stands with you in your pain. Write it on a Post-it or note card and set it in a place where you will see it throughout your day.

INSPIRATION: "The battles that count aren't the ones for gold medals. The struggles within yourself—the invisible, inevitable battles inside all of us—that's where it's at."

—JESSE OWENS, four-time gold medalist in track-and-field at the 1936 Olympics

NOTES FROM COACH SHAWN: Have some flexibility with your training schedule based on how your body feels and the demands of your life. Listen to your body when it needs an additional easy day or even a complete rest day. This will be good for you, both physically and mentally.

Use the space below to jot down some notes about your daily workouts or goals.

SUNDAY   MILES

MONDAY   MILES

TUESDAY   MILES _____

WEDNESDAY   MILES _____

THURSDAY   MILES _____

FRIDAY   MILES _____

SATURDAY   MILES _____

TOTAL MILES _____

49

RESTING AS PART OF TRAINING

Yes, my soul, find rest in God; my hope comes from him.

Psalm 62:5

FAITH FUEL

You may know it all too well. When the alarm sounds on Monday morning and you feel like your head barely hit the pillow. Your body creaks and groans when you try to will it to wake up, to step into the light of a new week. You bargain with time, begging her for a few extra minutes to savor rest.

This morning I was grateful for the moon, which gently greeted me when I made it outside for my run. It sat glowing in a bed of pastel blues and pinks—just a hint of color inviting me farther, not blinding me with the week's expectations.

I gave myself permission this morning for a slow, worshipful run. I'm cautiously inching back to exercise after the back injury I endured a few weeks ago. No time trials, no pacing, no paying attention to the clock. Just run and savor, I told myself. Just listen to God's whisper. I heard doves cooing. I stopped to take pictures of the sea of white roses on the corner. I marveled at the purple crepe myrtles in my neighbor's front yard.

I'm usually the girl who likes to shoot out of the starting blocks. My enthusiasm carries me from task to task. But this summer I'm learning to dance to a new rhythm. I'm not apologizing for a slower pace. I'm training my body and my soul to rest in new ways.

Perhaps one of the most meaningful things Shawn has taught me is the power of rest. When Shawn and I first started dating, we had a conversation that went a little like this:

"Soooo, what do you do on the weekends?" I asked him.

"Well, I wake up early on Saturday mornings and I go for a bike ride for a few hours, then I come home and eat a big breakfast and take a long nap," he said. "On Sundays, I get up early and go on my long runs, then I come home and eat, then get ready for church and usher for the two morning services. After church, I come home and take a nap."

I remember thinking to myself, *Well, buddy, that's going to change if you invite me and my three daughters into your life.*

Shawn is an athlete and a coach. Over his lifetime, Shawn has competed in six Ironman races (which includes a 2.4 mile swim, 112-mile bike ride, and 26.2-mile run) and dozens of marathons. Rest is not optional for him; it's an integral part of training. When he joined our family, he helped shift our attitudes about rest.

Studies show that rest days are just as important as intense workout days for runners. Our muscles need time for recovery and regeneration. According to physician Saundra Dalton-Smith, author of *Sacred Rest*, humans need seven kinds of rest: physical, mental, social, creative, emotional, spiritual, and sensory. Most people rest only in one or two areas and then wonder why they still feel exhausted.[1]

In the Psalms, David talks about the soul rest only God provides. "Truly my soul finds rest in God; my salvation comes from him"

(Psalm 62:1). David seems to be preaching truth to himself that God is the one who brings true rest.

The same phrase, "find rest in God," is echoed in Psalm 62:5: "Yes, my soul, find rest in God; my hope comes from him." God is both our salvation and our hope. The Hebrew word used in this context for rest actually means "silence" related to "being quiet, still or ceasing."[2] This echoes Psalm 46:10 that says, "Be still, and know that I am God." We are to stop moving, stop striving, stop fighting, and simply rest in silence and in knowing we can trust God.

Shawn led our family by example and encouragement. In the early days of our marriage, he gave me permission to rest. He congratulated me if I took a nap on the weekends. He helped me carve out time for trail runs, writing conferences, and weekend getaways with friends to refresh my mind and soul. We take naps together on Sunday afternoons as a regular part of our family rhythm. Shawn helped me move away from guilt when I took time to rest. Together we have been training our daughters to listen to their bodies and choose rest as well.

Friend, did you know you are invited to rest too? Give yourself permission today.

FAITH STEP: Take a "rest inventory" on your life. If humans need seven kinds of rest, including physical, mental, social, creative, emotional, spiritual, and sensory, how are you doing? Make a chart and jot down some ways you are resting in each area. If you have gaps in your chart, brainstorm ways you might rest in those categories. Add them to your schedule as it works for you.

INSPIRATION: "I often hear someone say I'm not a real runner. We are all runners, some just run faster than others. I never met a fake runner."

—BART YASSO, chief running officer for *Runner's World* magazine

NOTES FROM COACH SHAWN: Adequate rest and sleep are critical components to competing at a high level. When running, you are breaking your muscles and body down. It is during the rest periods that your body rebuilds and repairs itself into a stronger version of you.

Use the space below to jot down some notes about your daily workouts or goals.

SUNDAY   MILES _____

MONDAY   MILES _____

TUESDAY   MILES _____

WEDNESDAY   MILES _____

THURSDAY   MILES _____

FRIDAY   MILES _____

SATURDAY   MILES _____

TOTAL MILES _____

50

DEALING WITH
DISAPPOINTMENT

"Remember not the former things, nor consider the things of
old. Behold, I am doing a new thing; now it springs forth, do
you not perceive it? I will make a way in the wilderness and
rivers in the desert."

Isaiah 43:18–19 ESV

FAITH FUEL

As mentioned earlier, a few years ago I ran the Chicago Marathon
for my fortieth birthday. Nineteen family members and friends
traveled from the West Coast to Chicago to run or cheer me on. I
diligently trained for months for this race with my hubby, Shawn,
and my running buddy Marina. We put in the long runs, the core
training, and the speed workouts to prepare for race day. I was on
track for a personal record in the marathon.

Then race day finally arrived.

I knew from the start that I wasn't feeling great. Despite being surrounded by such an awesome "cloud of witnesses" and my people cheering for me along the course, I couldn't find my pace. My stomach felt wonky and necessitated two bathroom stops. (I *hate* stopping for the bathroom during a race.) By mile fifteen, my lower back was screaming and my right foot felt tingly and numb. The sun was beating down on my back. I felt parched.

Marina said she was going on ahead and would meet me at the finish. I didn't blame her one bit. I probably would have done the same if the tables were turned. However, the competitive side of me had a hard time accepting that I couldn't push harder to stay with her like I had during training.

My self-talk turned negative. I felt like a tangled mess. My sin was in my attitude, my comparing, my jealousy, my shame. I wanted to just lie down in the middle of the street and ugly-cry.

By God's grace and the steady coaching of my husband, I finished the 26.2 miles without stopping or walking, but I was much slower than I expected. The physical pain took its toll. Even though I fought to the finish line that day, I still felt defeated. I was deeply disappointed with my time and in my body.

All of us will face deep disappointment at some point in our lives. We often perceive that others are disappointed in us when our own unmet expectations are at the root. I have learned that sometimes I need to give myself space to grieve my own hopes and dreams before I can move on.

Isaiah 43:18–19 says, "Remember not the former things, nor consider the things of old. Behold, I am doing a new thing; now it springs forth, do you not perceive it? I will make a way in the wilderness and rivers in the desert" (ESV). This prophecy was meant to encourage the remnant of Jews seeking to return to Jerusalem from Babylon. These words were also meant to impart courage to us today.

This passage can be divided into three parts as listeners are urged to remember not, to behold, and to look to the unexpected future. Verse 18 urges us to "remember not the former things," or not to dwell on the past. When we experience deep disappointment, sometimes we can get stuck there. But there is a time to move on, to see something new. "Behold" invites us to pause and discern, to observe "the new thing" God is doing.

We have this hope—promised by God—that "springs forth" into the future. In verse 19, we can "behold" a picture of this hope: "I will make a way in the wilderness and rivers in the desert." This is strong imagery that paints a picture of the unexpected. We wouldn't expect water in the wilderness or rivers in the desert. But just as God parted the Red Sea and provided water for the Israelites in the wilderness, in the book of Exodus, He makes a way forward through our disappointment.

Admittedly, it was hard to return to running after that experience in Chicago. My body ached, but even more, my soul ached with the memory of disappointment. Eventually, I started out slow, recalibrating my body, and then embracing running again. I believed and perceived God was doing something new within me. Friend, let's allow our disappointments and failures to propel us forward rather than holding us back today.

FAITH STEP: Have you ever been deeply disappointed? What were your unmet expectations in that situation? How did you move forward with God's help? If you are still in that process, give yourself space to grieve and then pray for God to make a way for you to move forward.

INSPIRATION: "I've always been good at putting things behind me—I fall apart, do my crying bit, and then put it away and move on."

—PAULA RADCLIFFE, British marathoner and former women's world record holder

NOTES FROM COACH SHAWN: After a devastating race result, take a two- to four-week break from structured training to give your body and mind a chance to recover and regroup. Cross-train by swimming or cycling, or try running easy, without caring about pace, in a beautiful, scenic place to inspire and reinvigorate your passion for running.

Use the space below to jot down some notes about your daily workouts or goals.

SUNDAY	MILES ____

MONDAY	MILES ____

TUESDAY	MILES ____

WEDNESDAY	MILES ____

THURSDAY	MILES ____

FRIDAY	MILES ____

SATURDAY	MILES ____

TOTAL MILES ____

51

FINISHING WELL

However, I consider my life worth nothing to me; my only aim is to finish the race and complete the task the Lord Jesus has given me—the task of testifying to the good news of God's grace.

Acts 20:24

FAITH FUEL

The first marathon I ever ran was the Rock 'n' Roll Marathon in San Diego. My late husband, Ericlee, promised he would help me train and get me to the finish line. I was a young married girl in my twenties. I thought training for a marathon together sounded like the perfect way to spend more time with my husband. What I didn't realize was that he would be the one doing most of the talking, and I would be the one breathing and trying to keep up.

I was still a sprinter at heart. As an athlete, I specialized in the 400m and 300m hurdles. The farthest I had ever run was a 10K, so 26.2 miles felt nothing short of daunting.

Ericlee was an inspiring and determined coach. He wrote up a three-month training plan for us, which included short runs, longer runs, a half-marathon race, and some cross-training. We logged lots of hours together running the streets and trails of our city. One thing Ericlee encouraged me to do while I ran was to memorize Scripture.

I chose Acts 20:24 as my special verse during that season. With each mile, I memorized a few more words and phrases. We would recite the verse out loud to each other as we ran. I found that especially when I felt fatigued or the summer sun was beating down on me, these words helped me find the strength to keep going.

This verse is part of Paul's farewell address to the Ephesian elders. Paul models humility for the leaders as he anticipates the hardship that he will encounter in Jerusalem. He offers this eternal perspective: "However, I consider my life worth nothing to me; my only aim is to finish the race and complete the task the Lord Jesus has given me—the task of testifying to the good news of God's grace" (Acts 20:24). Once again, Paul is comparing life to a running race. With these words, Paul invited his audience and us today to run focused on the finish line. He highlighted our purpose to testify or bear witness to the truth of the gtospel.

Just a few months after Ericlee died, I ran my first trail race. As I ran solo through the rolling hills and across the rocky terrain, the words of Acts 20:24 began to run through my mind. And more than a decade later, this verse has helped me persevere to the finish line.

Friend, we never know how many races we have left in us. As we run through each new day, let's complete our assignment as Paul says—to testify and share with others about God's grace.

FAITH STEP: What do you think it means to finish well in a running race? What are some ways you can "testify to the gospel of God's grace in your own life"? Write or type out the words to Acts 20:24. Take them with you on your next training run to read over and memorize.

INSPIRATION: "I always want to give more than I gave yesterday."

—ALLYSON FELIX, American Olympic sprint champion

NOTES FROM COACH SHAWN: When at the starting line, you often get the race you trained for. If your training didn't go as planned and you missed several key workouts or had injuries, adjust your time goals for the race. On race day, maximize the fitness you do have, but don't expect your body to perform at a level that you didn't train it for.

Use the space below to jot down some notes about your daily workouts or goals.

SUNDAY   MILES _____

MONDAY   MILES _____

TUESDAY   MILES _____

WEDNESDAY   MILES _____

THURSDAY   MILES _____

FRIDAY   MILES _____

SATURDAY   MILES _____

                                            TOTAL MILES _____

52

RUNNING THE ULTRAMARATHON

But we have this treasure in jars of clay, to show that the surpassing power belongs to God and not to us. We are afflicted in every way, but not crushed; perplexed, but not driven to despair; persecuted, but not forsaken; struck down, but not destroyed; always carrying in the body the death of Jesus, so that the life of Jesus may also be manifested in our bodies.

2 Corinthians 4:7–10 ESV

FAITH FUEL

Some days do feel like a glorious sprint to the finish line, but I'm learning that life is more often like an ultramarathon.

Ultras are gaining popularity these days as more and more people look to push themselves to the next level. There are two types of ultramarathons: those that cover a specific distance (anywhere from 31–100+ miles), and those that last for a predetermined amount of time. My body aches and creaks just thinking about running these extensive distances and hours; they require not just physical stamina, but incredible mental toughness as well.

Then I think about how Jesus was the ultimate ultrarunner. In His last week of earthly ministry, Jesus ran the ultra-race of a lifetime. Jesus told His disciples to prepare for the Passover feast. During that meal, Jesus washed His disciples' feet as a radical expression of His deep love for them. He held up the bread and wine and explained that His body and blood would be offered up for each one of them.

After the Passover meal, Jesus took His disciples to the Mount of Olives for His final message to them. He promised to send them the Holy Spirit to counsel, guide, and coach them. Jesus then journeyed on to Gethsemane, where He agonized in prayer. The course grew challenging here. As He finished praying, His disciple Judas came and betrayed Him with a kiss; He was arrested and taken to Annas, where He was sentenced to death for claiming to be the Son of God.

Pontius Pilate, the Roman governor, tried to convince the Jewish leaders and people of Jesus' innocence, but a mob gathered. In a poor attempt to appease the crowd, Pilate had Jesus stripped, mocked, and severely beaten. The mob was not satisfied and called for Jesus' crucifixion. This was not even the hardest leg of Jesus' final race.

Crucifixion was reserved for the worst and lowest criminals. The soldiers stripped Jesus and put a scarlet robe on Him. They twisted together a crown of thorns—a great contrast to the laurel crowns awarded to Olympians—and pressed it into His head. They spit on Him and struck Him. Then He had to climb a great hill He had created, where His hands and feet were nailed to a cross.

The cross was hoisted up in the darkness and Jesus hung there, crying out, "My God, my God, why have you forsaken me?" Someone offered Him a sponge of sour wine, but He wouldn't drink it. He was beyond dehydration. This was worse than hitting the wall. He exhaled His last breath. This was the end.

Or so some thought.

The earth quaked with sorrow. His body was brought to a tomb that was closely guarded and covered with a heavy stone. Jesus was separated from His Father for three days. Can you imagine the loneliness and betrayal He endured on that journey?

On the third day, an angel of the Lord descended from heaven and went to the tomb. He rolled back the stone and revealed to the women who waited that Jesus was not there. Light refracted in all directions. He was resurrected, claiming victory over death.

Shortly afterward, Jesus himself appeared to the women. They fell at His feet and worshiped Him—their King, their Savior, the greatest ultrarunner of all time. They were witnesses to His race wounds and His healing. Then He sent those women to tell the others. And they ran.

Running reminds us of Jesus' journey. Running is hard—physically, emotionally, and mentally. But we know that doing hard things means we are following in Jesus' footsteps. Paul says this about following Him in the hard things: "But we have this treasure in jars of clay, to show that the surpassing power belongs to God and not to us. We are afflicted in every way, but not crushed; perplexed, but not driven to despair; persecuted, but not forsaken; struck down, but not destroyed; always carrying in the body the death of Jesus, so that the life of Jesus may also be manifested in our bodies" (2 Corinthians 4:7–10 ESV).

When we run this life race, we will encounter trials, but we carry in our hearts the knowledge that Jesus himself ran this arduous race to the finish. In our weakness, He imparts strength to us so that we, too, might taste the glory of the finish line.

FAITH STEP: Do you believe Jesus ran the ultimate race when He died and rose again? Have you ever asked Him to be your personal Savior? Have you ever confessed your sin and brokenness to Him? Take time to pray today and to invite Him into your heart. If you already know Him in a personal way, write out a thank-you to Him for the suffering He endured on your behalf.

INSPIRATION: "I tell people you should do one marathon in your lifetime. After that, it's optional. That's because running that 26.2-mile distance can teach you things that running a half marathon or a 10K or 5K race can't. If you can overcome those challenges to get ready for a marathon and get to that finish line, it changes your life. You are going to find something you never thought you were capable of doing."

—MEB KEFLEZIGHI, American marathoner who is the only person to win an Olympic medal, the Boston Marathon, and the New York City Marathon

NOTES FROM COACH SHAWN: Good form can transform your speed, reduce injuries, and increase your running enjoyment. Run tall with your hips high and a slight forward lean from your ankles rather than your waist. This will help you breathe easier and give your legs greater range of motion. Keep your shoulders relaxed while pumping your arms forward and backward with your elbows bent at about a 90-degree angle. The faster you pump your arms, the faster your feet will move.

Use the space below to jot down some notes about your daily workouts or goals.

SUNDAY   MILES _____

MONDAY   MILES _____

TUESDAY   MILES _____

WEDNESDAY   MILES _____

THURSDAY   MILES _____

FRIDAY   MILES _____

SATURDAY   MILES _____

                                    TOTAL MILES _____

HOW TO FORM
A RUNNING GROUP

We call ourselves the Go Mama Runners. We are a motley crew of mamas who meet up when our schedules allow for weekend runs. We are all shapes and sizes and speeds. Some walk, some jog, some run, and some race. What we all have in common is a love for the outdoors and a pull in our hearts for connection.

We wake up before the sun lifts her head on Saturday morning and pack a handful of us into my hybrid SUV. Sometimes we take two or three cars if there's a bigger group. We make a beeline for the Winchell Cove Trail, about twenty minutes from my house, in search of adventure, fresh air, community, and a healthy dose of God's glory through His creation.

There's something magical about running free on a winding trail with friends. This particular single-track trail follows the curve around Millerton Lake in central California. We run on the trail above while water laps at the shore below. I am mesmerized again and again by the waves of golden grasses undulating over the hills, the cerulean blue sky, and the branches of the trees dancing toward heaven.

I love the way our conversations wander as we run. We delve deeper into topics when we have a winding trail before us. On the trail, we catch up, talk about schooling options, and dish about dreams, relationships, politics, or theology. Too often our everyday conversations are interrupted and fragmented when kids are in tow. That's why these weekend trail runs have become precious.

God created each one of us for community. The Greek word for community is *koinonia*, also meaning "fellowship, connection, participation, and partnership." Through the years, I've discovered that running is often a richer experience when we go together. Running with a partner, team, or group helps provide motivation, accountability, and connection.

The author of Hebrews puts it this way: "And let us consider how we may spur one another on toward love and good deeds, not giving up meeting together, as some are in the habit of doing, but encouraging one another—and all the more as you see the Day approaching" (Hebrews 10:24–25). In community, we spur each other on to the finish line. If one member is struggling, another mamarunner may come alongside and encourage her to keep going.

I've been a part of and led many different teams and groups through the years. I'd like to offer some practical tips and things to consider when forming a running/walking group:

1. **Choose a way to communicate that makes sense for your group.** Our Go Mama Runner group formed a Facebook group. We use that space to post meeting dates, maps, links to races we are interested in, and articles about running and gear. You might consider using an email list, a texting group, Voxer, or the Marco Polo app.

2. **Pick a regular time to meet.** When Shawn and I coach the Remember Haiti Half Marathon team, we host midweek workouts at a local track, and long runs on Saturdays from our house.

3. **Form pace groups.** Within your group, there may be a small group of people who run or walk at the same pace. It's good to help people connect with their pace group early on so they have someone they can run or walk alongside. In our Go Mama Runner group, we tend to have a group

of fast trail runners, a medium group, and then a group of walkers/joggers. Even if everyone does not have a partner, it's nice to know someone is in front of you or behind you. This is an important safety measure and gives the opportunity for team members to encourage one another.

4. **Consider ordering team swag.** We order the same signature gold dri-FIT T-shirts every year for our Remember Haiti team, and we wear them on race day so our team and fans can identify the runners/walkers who are part of our team. I've been a part of other teams that have ordered special tank tops, hats, or even long socks to help identify the team and create camaraderie.

5. **Start your run with a devotional time.** You might consider using this devotional with your group. Have one team member read a devotional at the start. Another team member could pray for the group before they head out on a run/walk. You might gather at the finish to cool down and discuss the questions, or connect through your online or text group by posting comments and feedback. Something like this helps unite the team around a common goal, thought, or Bible passage.

6. **Pick a race and train together.** Throughout the year, our Go Mama Runner group picks a few trail races to train for together. Shawn might put together a training plan for a few of us, and we try to meet up regularly to work out or train on hills together. It's not a requirement for every member, but it's a fun excuse to plan a trip together, and it gives us all motivation to reach a goal.

RUNNING FOR A CAUSE

In 2009, my late husband, Ericlee, and I were preparing for a move from Fresno, California, to Pignon, Haiti, where we had plans to help direct a nonprofit organization. Part of our preparation involved fundraising for our travels and living expenses. Since we were both runners, my husband suggested a fundraiser that would use our passion and talent. We decided to run a local half marathon and get sponsors jog-a-thon style. What we didn't anticipate is that seventeen of our friends would sign up to run the race and fundraise with us.

The Remember Haiti Half Marathon Fundraiser team was born in Summer 2009. Ericlee helped develop workouts, and together we coached the team to the finish line. We discovered the power of embarking on a goal like this in community.

Over the last decade, our team has helped raise thousands of dollars for various projects that benefit friends in the northern mountains of Haiti. We have helped dig wells for schools so they could offer fresh water for kids. We have supplied paint and money for laborers to paint orphanages. We have helped build and supply a kitchen so schoolkids could have regular meals daily. We have raised funds to start a running group for youth and offer them running shoes and jerseys. These are just a few examples of the impactful projects we have had the privilege of being a part of through the years.

We encourage you to consider gathering a group of your friends and running for a cause. Signing up for a race together and raising money for a project can be a great motivator and community builder. Here are a few quick tips:

1. Research and pick a project, cause, or nonprofit to support through your fundraising. Consider something local or a national cause you are personally passionate about.

2. Reach out to the director of communications for that organization and share about your plans. Ask about ways you can partner with what their organization might be doing. Make sure to develop a clear avenue through which people can give donations. Many people care about tax-deductible

donations, so you might inquire about the organization's tax ID number to include in your letters.

3. Gather general details about the organization and their work to share with your team. You might put together a list of bullet points or collect brochures or other promotional materials they already use.

4. Begin to recruit people for your team. Talk to friends, co-workers, neighbors, and others who might be interested in gathering around a goal and/or getting in shape. Share about your passion, the project, and how they might get involved with chasing this goal with you.

5. Draft a support letter. Describe who you are, a little about your team, the organization you are supporting, and the specific project you are raising funds for. Make this an editable document so teammates can personalize the letter and send to their own sponsors.

6. Set goals and deadlines as a team for fundraising. You might make a dollar goal or require each team member to send out a certain number of support letters. Don't forget to connect with local businesses. They often have a budget set aside for supporting causes like this.

7. Develop a workout plan for the team. You might use workouts in this book or look up some online if you do not have your own coaching experience. Plan to meet with your team regularly to walk/run/work out together. Once- or twice-a-week meetups are a huge encouragement.

8. Order team T-shirts or tank tops. This is a fun way to unite and reward the team. You might ask a local business owner or group of businesses to sponsor your team and include their logos on your T-shirt for advertising.

9. Plan a team dinner for the week of the race or the night before. This can be an opportunity for people to invite

their families. You can celebrate the work you all have put in training for the race and raising funds.

10. Meet up on race day for a team photo and to pray together before the race. You might also consider making a spot to meet after the race to cheer each other on and celebrate team members crossing the finish line.

TIPS FOR MEMORIZING SCRIPTURE WHILE RUNNING

Most of us would not boast that we are good at memorizing Scripture. It's a practice that might feel rote or out-of-date, but there are many benefits to memorizing and meditating on God's Word regularly.

Deuteronomy 11:18 reminds us to "Fix these words of mine in your hearts and minds; tie them as symbols on your hands and bind them on your foreheads." In other words, we are to make Scripture and the Bible's teachings a part of our daily routine. One way to do this is by memorizing Scripture while running.

Many of us feel defeated before we even begin memorizing Scripture. Sometimes we just need a goal and some creative ways to tackle the task. That's why I'd like to offer up some helpful tips and strategies for learning verses while running:

1. Choose a time frame to learn a verse or passage. You might tackle one verse a week or a month. Put it on your calendar and share the goal with a friend so you feel accountable.

2. Start small and chunk it up. Choose your verse or passage and then divide it into sections to learn over time. You might use colored markers to highlight different sections or write it out.

3. Print out Scriptures to take with you. Slip the paper in your pocket so you can pull it out for quick reference when

you're running. Another option is to create or find a lock screen for your phone so you can easily access the verse you are working on.

4. Listen to the verses on a Bible app like YouVersion. Sometimes listening to the whole chapter can give context to a passage so you understand the meaning. You might listen to different translations or versions as well.

5. Read over the Scripture passage when you're taking a water break. You will need water breaks on longer runs/walks, so this is the perfect time to go back and read over your Scripture so you have the words in your mind.

6. Visualize the passage as you run. This is a great strategy to help you meditate on the words and meaning of the Scripture. What do they look like? What are the shape of the words? How do these words apply to situations in your life?

7. Set the words to music. You might search for songs or make up your own tune to help you memorize the verses. I have lots of Scriptures in my head as an adult that I learned as songs when I was a child.

8. Share your Scripture with a partner or group. Carve out time with a friend to say the Scripture to each other before or after your run. Quiz and encourage each other on the journey to hide God's Word in your hearts.

WARM-UP DRILLS
FOR RUNNERS

(from Coach Shawn)

DRILL DESCRIPTIONS

Skipping

Skipping will increase your heart rate, loosen your legs, and engage your hip flexors, calves, and feet.

Forward skipping: Skip forward, driving one knee up and then the other. Step, hop, step, hop, and repeat. Be relaxed and skip like when you were a kid. Coordinate your arms and your legs so that your right arm drives up as your left knee drives up, and vice versa. Keep the heel of your driving leg underneath your knee rather than kicking it out in front of you. Skip forward for 20 meters.

Backward skipping: Skipping backward requires a little bit more coordination than moving forward. The form mimics forward skipping, except you are moving backward. It is the same pattern of step, hop, step, hop, and repeat. Skip backward for 20 meters.

Hip Flexors

Hip flexor muscles are critical to running and are often overlooked. They help initiate your stride and lift your feet. Your hip flexors are a group of muscles positioned in front of your hips. Strong hip flexors will help your stride stay steady throughout your run.

Straight-leg march: Stay tall and kick your right leg straight up as you reach forward to touch your right toe with your left hand. Repeat with your left leg and right hand. Straight-leg march for 20 meters.

High knees: Drive each knee up and down quickly as you move forward. Use a short stride and have your feet quickly respond and push off the ground. Drive your arms back and forth with your elbows bent at a 90-degree angle. Stay tall without leaning backward. Focus on fast feet and getting your knees up instead of moving forward. Do high knees for 20 meters.

Quads and Hamstrings

Your quadriceps are the front muscles of your upper thigh. They are important for propelling yourself forward. Your hamstrings are the muscles in the back of your upper leg. These muscles help drive your foot forward after toe-off.

Walking quad stretch: As you take a step with your left foot, reach behind you with your right hand and pull your right heel toward your butt. Keep your right knee underneath your torso rather than pulling it off to the side. At the same time, reach up with your left hand toward the sky. Stay tall and do not lean forward at the waist. Repeat this for stepping with your right foot and using your left hand to pull your left heel toward your butt. Perform this walking quad stretch for 20 meters.

Butt kickers: Stand tall with your feet together. Rise up on to the balls of your feet and lean slightly forward from your ankles. As you fall forward, and take a step with your left foot, quickly drive your right heel toward your butt. Next, take a step with your right foot and drive your left heel toward your butt. Repeat this sequence to wake up your hamstrings for the run ahead. Do butt kickers for 20 meters.

Calves

Perform your calf exercises before and after each run. Strong calves will help you push off with each step. Perform these calf drills on your strength/core days as well.

Toe hops: Shift your weight to the balls of your feet with your feet shoulder-width apart and your legs straight (although your knees should not be locked). Hop up and down by flexing your ankles and squeezing your calf muscles. All the motion should be initiated by your calves, ankles, and toes. Do not use much of your quadriceps for this exercise. Perform 1 set of 20 reps for this exercise.

Go-to move (GTM): The GTM is my favorite drill and my only move on the dance floor, much to my wife's chagrin. It is similar to toe hops, but allow one knee to drive up while you hop on the other foot. At the same time, pump your arms with your elbow bent at a 90-degree angle. As your right knee drives up, your left arm pumps forward. As your right foot hits the ground, your left arm drives backward. Repeat this drill, letting your left knee drive up. Do 15 reps of the GTM for each leg.

Calf raises: Stand with your forefeet on a step with your heels hanging off the step. Position your feet shoulder-width apart and parallel with your toes pointing forward. Keep your knees straight but not locked. Slowly lower yourself so that your heels drop below the top level of the step and then raise yourself up onto your toes. Squeeze your calves to get higher on your toes. Perform 2 sets of 10 reps with 20 seconds rest between sets.

LEG SWINGS (GLUTES AND HIPS)

Leg swings loosen up your hips and increase your range of motion. They also engage your glute muscles, which are your speed muscles. Strong glutes help you sprint faster.

Forward/backward swings: Stand upright and keep one leg straight (but not locked) and the other leg bent at the knee at a 30-degree angle. Engage your glute muscles to swing the bent leg back and forth so that the ball of your foot lightly scrapes (paws) the ground directly beneath where you are standing. Swing your leg back and forth for your full range of motion. Perform this exercise next to a wall or post that you can hold on to with one hand for balance. Swing the inside leg next to the wall or post with the outside leg stationary. Keep the swinging movement controlled. Perform 2 sets of 10 with each leg and aim for full range of motion without overextending yourself.

Side-to-side swings: Stand facing about 3 feet away from a wall and put both hands flat against the wall at about chest level. If there is a post or railing at about waist height, that can be used as well. Stand elevated on the ball of your left foot while swinging your right leg side-to-side across your body. Keep your swinging leg bent at the knee at a 30-degree angle. Keep the swinging movement controlled. Perform 2 sets of 10 with each leg and aim for full range of motion without overextending yourself.

ARM SWINGS

Your arms are the accelerator in running. The faster you pump your arms, the faster your legs will move. Running speed is a function of stride rate (how fast you take steps) and stride length (how long each step is). Increase your stride rate by moving your arms faster. Increase your stride length by pumping your arms with a larger range of motion. As a big tip, you run faster when you are relaxed and can freely move your arms, so keep your shoulders and arms relaxed throughout your run.

Arm swings: Position your feet shoulder-width apart and stand tall. Shift your weight slightly onto your forefeet. Your heels may come up ever so slightly, but do not stand on your toes. Relax your shoulders and bend your elbows to roughly a 90-degree angle. Your arms should be comfortable, so the angle at your elbows may be a little less or more than 90 degrees. Pump your arms forward and backward, not side-to-side. Think of having a string pulling your elbows back. Also, as you pump your arms, look forward rather than at the ground.

As you practice arm swings, notice how when you pump your right arm back, your left hip shifts forward. Similarly, as your left arm swings back, your right hip moves forward. Your arms initiate your opposite hip to move forward, which in turn initiates your hip flexors to engage and lift your legs forward.

Pump your arms slowly at first and then steadily speed up the pace. Perform 2 sets of easy swinging for 15 seconds, moderate for 10 seconds, and fast for 5 seconds.

CORE EXERCISES FOR RUNNERS

Below are some core exercises to choose from. Ideally, you will do the entire routine at least two to three times a week. If you are short on time, perform at least the first three (leg raises, crunches, plank routine) and the lower-back extensions (or Supermans). You may need to build up to handle the full reps and the entire routine, but that is okay. Do as much as you can to start with and then build from there. Remember, you need to walk before you can run and run before you can soar!

1. Leg raises (15 reps): Lie on your back and with straight legs and together, raise them both to a vertical position so your body is in an "L" position. Slowly lower them. Keep your lower back pressed firmly against the floor, and do not rush.

2. Crunches (15 reps): Lie on your back with your feet flat. Stick both arms straight, fully extended vertically up in the air. Raise your torso, engaging your abdominals while trying to elevate your fingertips as high as possible into the air. Do not rush and focus on using your abs.

3. Plank routine (2 minutes total)—30 seconds regular, 30 seconds right side, 30 seconds left side, 30 seconds regular (no rest in between switching positions). When in the normal plank position, keep your shoulder lined up over your elbows and try to keep a flat back and your butt low

but your abdominals engaged. When doing the side plank, stick the arm not supporting your weight either vertically in the air or overhead as if you are taking a stroke during swimming.

4. Scissors (15 reps): Lie on your back and, keeping your legs straight, set your left leg 2 inches off the ground and your right leg pointing straight in the air at a 90-degree angle to your body. Scissors your legs so that your left leg switches to vertical and your right leg drops to 2 inches off the ground. One full scissor equals one rep. Pause briefly in between scissors. This move works your hip flexors.

5. Heels to the heavens (15 reps): Lie on your back with your legs together and straight, pointing in the sky. Keep your feet flat (i.e., don't point your toes upward). Roll your hips off the floor by using so that your heels are pressing directly upward. This move works your lower abdominals.

6. Bicycles (15 forward, 15 reverse): Sit on your butt and lean back a little, keeping your lower abdominals engaged. Elevate both legs and "pedal" in the air forward for 15 times and back 15 times. Circle the feet so that each foot passes by the ankle of the other foot. This really engages the hip flexors.

7. Lower-back extensions/Supermans (2 sets of 10): If you're at a gym, you will probably be able to use a low-back extension machine. Perform your reps with your arms folded across your chest or extended out in front of you. If you don't have access to this machine, perform Supermans: Lie on your stomach with your arms and legs extended in an X. Raise your arms and legs upward at the same time. Pause briefly, then relax. Strengthening your lower back and core will help tremendously with your running form so you don't slouch and will encourage you to run "tall."

WALK, RUN, SOAR 5K

GOAL RACE:

A) _____

B) _____

C) Finish

THEMES:

A) Stride rate and speed

B) Consistency

C) Focus on and do what you can do. Adapt workouts as needed.

TOTAL MILEAGE: 201.1 MILES

Comments:

1. Select A and B goals, since your C goal is to finish regardless the time. Your B goal is what you think you can accomplish with consistent training. Your A goal is a stretch goal and what you think you can accomplish if everything goes perfectly (training, weather, nutrition, etc.). A and B goals may be time based or even an attitude such as "finish with a smile."

2. Perform strength workouts on your own.

3. From a specialty running store, purchase quality running shoes that match your foot and running/walking style.

4. Eat less processed, sugary, and fried foods, fewer empty calories, and choose more wholesome items.

EASY = "Chatty Pace" — pace where you can still carry on a conversation

MODERATE = Difficult to talk and you need more focus

HARD = Fast as you can UNDER CONTROL

WEEK # EFFORT	MONDAY	TUESDAY	WEDNESDAY	THURSDAY	FRIDAY	SATURDAY	SUNDAY	TOTALS
1	Core/Strength Training	1 mile easy	Core/Strength Training	1.5 miles easy	Rest	2 miles easy	Rest	4.5
2	Core/Strength Training	1.5 miles easy	Core/Strength Training	1.5 miles easy	Rest	2 miles easy	Rest	5
3	Core/Strength Training	2 miles easy	Core/Strength Training	Track (2 miles) • 800 easy warmup • 4x400 moderate with 2-min rest • 800 easy cooldown	Rest	2.5 miles easy	Rest	6.5
4	Core/Strength Training	2.5 miles easy	Core/Strength Training	Track (2.5 miles) • 800 easy warmup • 3x400 moderate with 2-min rest • 2x400 hard with 3-min rest • 400 easy cooldown	Rest	3 miles easy	Rest	7

WEEK #	MONDAY	TUESDAY	WEDNESDAY	THURSDAY	FRIDAY	SATURDAY	SUNDAY	TOTALS
5	Core/Strength Training	2.5 miles easy	Core/Strength Training	Track (3 miles) • 800 easy warmup • 4x400 moderate with 1-min rest • 2x200 moderate with 1-min rest • 2x200 hard with 1-min rest • 800 easy cooldown	Rest	3.5 miles easy	Rest	8.5
6	Core/Strength Training	2.5 miles easy	Core/Strength Training	Track (3 miles) • 800 easy warmup • 3x400 easy with 1-min rest • 3x400 moderate with 2-min rest • 2x400 hard with 2-min rest • 800 easy cooldown	Rest	3 miles easy	Rest	8.5
7	Core/Strength Training	3 miles with 2nd mile easy and last mile moderate	Core/Strength Training	Track (3 miles) • 800 easy warmup • 3x400 easy with 1-min rest • 5x200 moderate with 1-min rest • 5x200 hard with 1-min rest • 800 easy cooldown	Rest	4 miles easy	Rest	10
8	Core/Strength Training	3 miles with 2nd mile moderate and last mile hard	Core/Strength Training	Track (3 miles) • 800 easy warmup • 600 moderate with 2-min rest • 600 hard with 3-min rest • 400 moderate with 2-min rest • 400 hard with 3-min rest • 200 moderate with 2-min rest • 200 hard with 3-min rest • 1200 easy cooldown	Rest	4 miles with 3rd mile moderate and last mile hard	Rest	13.5

WEEK #	MONDAY	TUESDAY	WEDNESDAY	THURSDAY	FRIDAY	SATURDAY	SUNDAY	TOTALS
9	Core/Strength Training	3 miles easy	Core/Strength Training	Track (3 miles) • 800 easy warmup • 4x400 moderate with 1-min rest • 4x300 moderate with 2-min rest • 4x200 hard with 2-min rest • 400 easy cooldown	Rest	3 miles easy	Rest	9
10	Core/Strength Training	3 miles easy with last mile hard	Core/Strength Training	Track (3 miles) • 800 easy warmup • 3x300 moderate with 1-min rest • 3x300 (200 moderate, 100 hard) with 2-min rest • 3x300 (100 mod, 200 hard) with 2-min rest • 3x300 hard with 2-min rest • 400 easy cooldown	Rest	4 miles with 2–3 moderate and last mile hard	Rest	10
11	Core/Strength Training	3 miles with 2nd mile moderate and last mile hard	Core/Strength Training	Track (4 miles) • 800 easy warmup • 800 moderate with 3-min rest • 4x600 moderate with 3-min rest • 4x400 hard with 2-min rest • 800 easy cooldown	Rest	4 miles easy	Rest	11
12	Core/Strength Training	3 miles with last mile hard	Core/Strength Training	Track (3 miles) • 800 easy warmup • 2x400 easy with 1-min rest • 2x400 moderate with 2-min rest • 2x400 hard with 2-min rest • 1600 easy cooldown	Rest	3 miles easy	Rest	9
13	Stretch	2 miles with last mile hard	Rest	2 miles with last mile moderate	Rest	**GOAL 5K RACE**	Rest	7.1

WALK, RUN, SOAR 10K

GOAL RACE:
A) _____
B) _____
C) Finish

THEMES:
A) Build up your run volume and long run
B) Consistency
C) Focus on and do what you can do. Adapt workouts as needed.

TOTAL MILEAGE: 201.1 MILES

Comments:
1. Select A and B goals, since your C goal is to finish regardless the time. Your B goal is what you think you can accomplish with consistent training. Your A goal is a stretch goal and what you think you can accomplish if everything goes perfectly (training, weather, nutrition, etc.). A and B goals may be time based or even an attitude such as "finish with a smile."
2. Perform strength workouts on your own.
3. From a specialty running store, purchase quality running shoes that match your foot and running/walking style.
4. Eat less processed, sugary, and fried foods, fewer empty calories, and choose more wholesome items.

EASY = "Chatty Pace" — pace where you can still carry on a conversation
MODERATE = Difficult to talk and you need more focus
HARD = Fast as you can UNDER CONTROL

WEEK #	MONDAY	TUESDAY	WEDNESDAY	THURSDAY	FRIDAY	SATURDAY	SUNDAY	TOTALS
1	Core/Strength Training	2 miles easy	Core/Strength Training	2 miles easy	Rest	2 miles easy	Rest	6
2	Core/Strength Training	2 miles easy	Core/Strength Training	Track (2 miles) • 800 easy warmup • 4x400 moderate with 2-min rest • 800 easy cooldown	Rest	3 miles easy	Rest	7
3	Core/Strength Training	2 miles easy with last mile moderate	Core/Strength Training	Track (2 miles) • 800 easy warmup • 2x400 easy with 1-min rest • 4x400 moderate with 2-min rest • 4x400 hard with 2-min rest • 800 easy cooldown	Rest	3.5 miles easy	Rest	8

WEEK #	MONDAY	TUESDAY	WEDNESDAY	THURSDAY	FRIDAY	SATURDAY	SUNDAY	TOTALS
4	Core/Strength Training	2.5 miles easy	Core/Strength Training	Track (2.5 miles) • 800 easy warmup • 2x400 moderate with 2-min rest • 2x600 hard • 600 easy cooldown	Rest	4 miles easy	Rest	9
5	Core/Strength Training	2.5 miles easy with last mile moderate	Core/Strength Training	Track (3 miles) • 800 easy warmup • 3x400 moderate with 2-min rest • 800 moderate with 3-min rest • 800 hard with 4 min rest • 400 hard • 800 easy cooldown	Rest	4.5 miles easy	Rest	10
6	Core/Strength Training	3 miles easy	Core/Strength Training	Track (3.5 miles) • 800 easy warmup • 2x400 moderate with 2-min rest • 3x800 moderate with 3-min rest • 800 hard • 800 easy cooldown	Rest	5 miles easy	Rest	11.5
7	Core/Strength Training	3 miles with 1st mile easy and last 2 miles moderate	Core/Strength Training	Track (3 miles) • 800 easy warmup • 2x400 easy with 1-min rest • 4x400 moderate with 2-min rest • 2x400 hard with 2-min rest • 1600 easy cooldown	Rest	5.5 miles easy	Rest	11.5
8	Core/Strength Training	4 miles easy	Core/Strength Training	Track (3.5 miles) • 800 easy warmup • 2x800 moderate with 3-min rest • 2x800 hard with 4-min rest • 2x400 hard with 3-min rest • 800 easy cooldown	Rest	6 miles easy	Rest	13.5

WEEK #	MONDAY	TUESDAY	WEDNESDAY	THURSDAY	FRIDAY	SATURDAY	SUNDAY	TOTALS
9	Core/Strength Training	4 miles with 3rd mile moderate and last mile hard	Core/Strength Training	Track (3.5 miles) • 800 easy warmup • 2x400 easy with 1-min rest • 2x400 moderate with 2-min rest • 2x600 moderate with 3-min rest • 2x600 hard with 4-min rest • 800 easy cooldown	Rest	7 miles easy	Rest	14.5
10	Core/Strength Training	4 miles easy	Core/Strength Training	Track (3.5 miles) • 800 easy warmup • 3x400 easy with 1-min rest • 3x400 moderate with 2-min rest • 4x400 hard with 3-min rest • 800 easy cooldown	Rest	5 miles easy	Rest	12.5
11	Core/Strength Training	5 miles easy	Core/Strength Training	Track (4 miles) • 800 easy warmup • 400 moderate with 2-min rest • 800 moderate with 3-min rest • 1200 moderate with 4-min rest • 1200 hard with 4-min rest hard with 4-min rest • 800 hard with 3-min rest • 400 hard • 800 easy cooldown	Rest	6 miles easy	Rest	15
12	Core/Strength Training	3 miles with 2nd mile moderate and last mile hard	Core/Strength Training	Track (3 miles) • 800 easy warmup • 2x400 easy with 1-min rest • 2x400 moderate with 2-min rest • 2x400 hard with 2-min rest • 1600 easy cooldown	Rest	4 miles easy	Rest	10
13	Stretch	3 miles with last mile hard	Rest	2 miles with last mile moderate	Rest	**GOAL 10K RACE**	Rest	11.2

WALK, RUN, SOAR HALF MARATHON

GOAL RACE:

A) _____

B) _____

C) Finish

THEMES:

A) Build up your run volume and long run

B) Stride rate and speed

C) Focus on and do what you can do. Adapt workouts as needed.

TOTAL MILEAGE: 201.1 MILES

Comments:

1. Select A and B goals, since your C goal is to finish regardless the time. Your B goal is what you think you can accomplish with consistent training. Your A goal is a stretch goal and what you think you can accomplish if everything goes perfectly (training, weather, nutrition, etc.). A and B goals may be time based or even an attitude such as "finish with a smile."

2. Perform strength workouts on your own.

3. From a specialty running store, purchase quality running shoes that match your foot and running/walking style.

4. Eat less processed, sugary, and fried foods, fewer empty calories, and choose more wholesome items.

EASY = "Chatty Pace" — pace where you can still carry on a conversation

MODERATE = Difficult to talk and you need more focus

HARD = Fast as you can UNDER CONTROL

WEEK #	MONDAY	TUESDAY	WEDNESDAY	THURSDAY	FRIDAY	SATURDAY	SUNDAY	TOTALS
1	Core/Strength Training	2 miles easy	Core/Strength Training	2.5 miles easy	Rest	3 miles easy	Rest	7.5
2	Core/Strength Training	3 miles easy	Core/Strength Training	Track (2.5 miles) • 800 easy warmup • 2x400 easy with 1-min rest • 2x400 moderate with 2-min rest • 2x400 hard with 2-min rest • 800 easy cooldown	Rest	4 miles easy	Rest	9.5
3	Core/Strength Training	3 miles easy with last mile moderate	Core/Strength Training	Track (3 miles) • 800 easy warmup • 3x400 easy with 1-min rest • 1x800 hard with 4-min rest • 1x600 moderate with 2-min rest • 1x600 hard • 800 easy cooldown	Rest	5 miles easy	Rest	11

WEEK #	MONDAY	TUESDAY	WEDNESDAY	THURSDAY	FRIDAY	SATURDAY	SUNDAY	TOTALS
4	Core/Strength Training	4 miles easy with last 2 miles moderate	Core/Strength Training	Track (3 miles) • 800 easy warmup • 2x400 easy with 1-min rest • 2x600 moderate with 3-min rest • 2x600 hard with 4-min rest • 800 easy cooldown	Rest	6 miles easy	Rest	13
5	Core/Strength Training	5 miles easy	Core/Strength Training	Track (3 miles) • 800 easy warmup • 2x400 moderate with 2-min rest • 2x800 moderate with 3-min rest • 800 hard • 800 easy cooldown	Rest	8 miles easy	Rest	16
6	Core/Strength Training	5 miles with 4th mile moderate and 5th mile hard	Core/Strength Training	Track (3 miles) • 800 easy warmup • 2x400 moderate with 2-min rest • 2x600 moderate with 2-min rest • 1200 hard • 800 easy cooldown	Rest	6 miles easy	Rest	14
7	Core/Strength Training	5 miles with 4th mile moderate and 5th mile hard	Core/Strength Training	Track (3.5 miles) • 800 easy warmup • 3x400 moderate with 1-min rest • 6x200 moderate with 1-min rest • 6x200 hard with 1-min rest • 1600 easy cooldown	Rest	9 miles easy	Rest	17.5
8	Core/Strength Training	6 miles easy	Core/Strength Training	Track (3.5 miles) • 800 easy warmup • 2x800 moderate with 3-min rest • 2x800 hard with 4-min rest • 2x400 hard with 3-min rest • 800 easy cooldown	Rest	10 miles easy	Rest	19.5

WEEK #	MONDAY	TUESDAY	WEDNESDAY	THURSDAY	FRIDAY	SATURDAY	SUNDAY	TOTALS
9	Core/Strength Training	6 miles easy with 4th and 5th miles moderate and last mile hard	Core/Strength Training	Track (3.5 miles) • 800 easy warmup • 2x800 moderate with 3-min rest • 2x800 hard with 4-min rest • 2x400 hard with 3-min rest • 800 easy cooldown	Rest	7 miles easy	Rest	16.5
10	Core/Strength Training	7 miles easy	Core/Strength Training	Track (3.5 miles) • 800 easy warmup • 3x400 easy with 1-min rest • 3x400 moderate with 2-min rest • 2x800 hard with 4-min rest • 800 easy cooldown	Rest	11 miles easy	Rest	21.5
11	Core/Strength Training	7 miles easy with last 3 miles moderate	Core/Strength Training	Track (4 miles) • 800 easy warmup • 400 moderate with 2-min rest • 800 moderate with 3-min rest • 1200 moderate with 4-min rest • 1200 hard with 4-min rest • 800 hard with 3-min rest • 400 hard • 800 easy cooldown	Rest	12 miles easy	Rest	23
12	Core/Strength Training	4 miles with 3rd mile moderate and last mile hard	Core/Strength Training	Track (3 miles) • 2x400 easy with 1-min rest • 2x400 moderate with 2-min rest • 2x400 hard with 2-min rest	Rest	7 miles easy	Rest	14
13	Stretch	3 miles with last mile hard	Rest	2 miles with last mile hard	Rest	**GOAL HALF MARATHON RACE**	Rest	18.1

APPENDIX 6

WALK, RUN, SOAR WEEKLY MILEAGE CHART

Create a line graph of your weekly mileage by putting a dot on the number of miles you run each week and connecting them with a line. Based on your weekly goal mileage, on the left-hand side select A, B, or C as the chart scale. If B and C do not accommodate your weekly mileage rate, choose A and write in an appropriate scale.

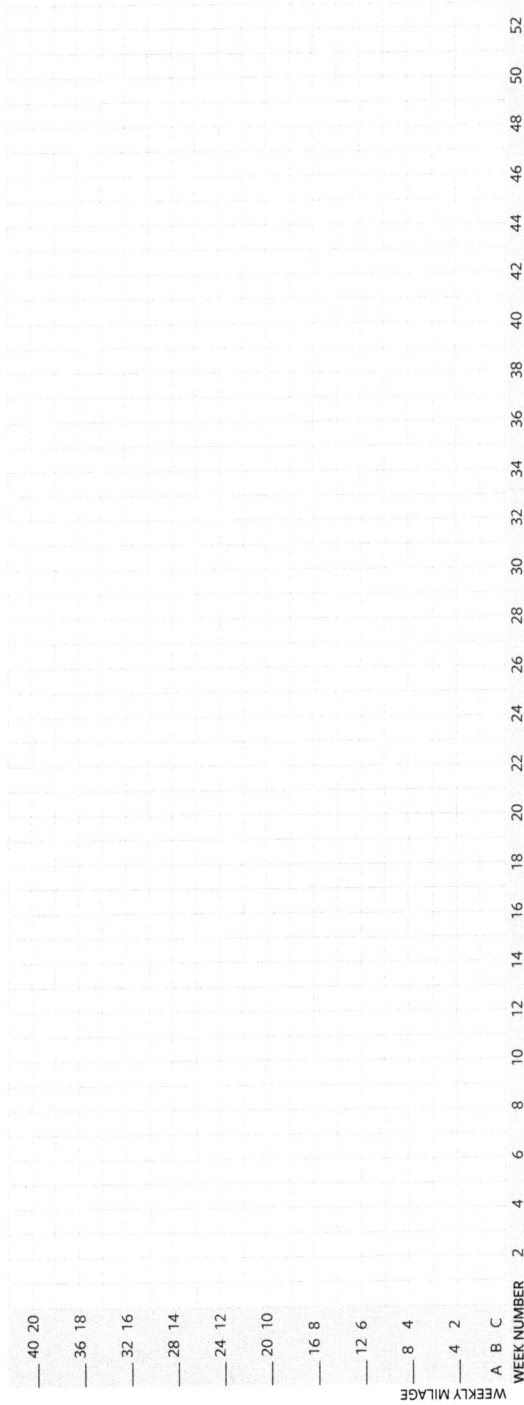

40	20		
36	18		
32	16		
28	14		
24	12		
20	10		
16	8		
12	6		
8	4		
4	2		
A	B	C	

WEEKLY MILAGE

WEEK NUMBER 2 4 6 8 10 12 14 16 18 20 22 24 26 28 30 32 34 36 38 40 42 44 46 48 50 52

WALK, RUN, SOAR ANNUAL MILEAGE CHART

Create a line graph of your annual cumulative mileage by putting a dot on the number of miles you run at the end of each week year-to-date and then connecting them with a line. Based on your annual goal mileage, on the left-hand side select A, B, or C as the chart scale. If B and C do not accommodate your annual mileage rate, choose A and write in an appropriate scale.

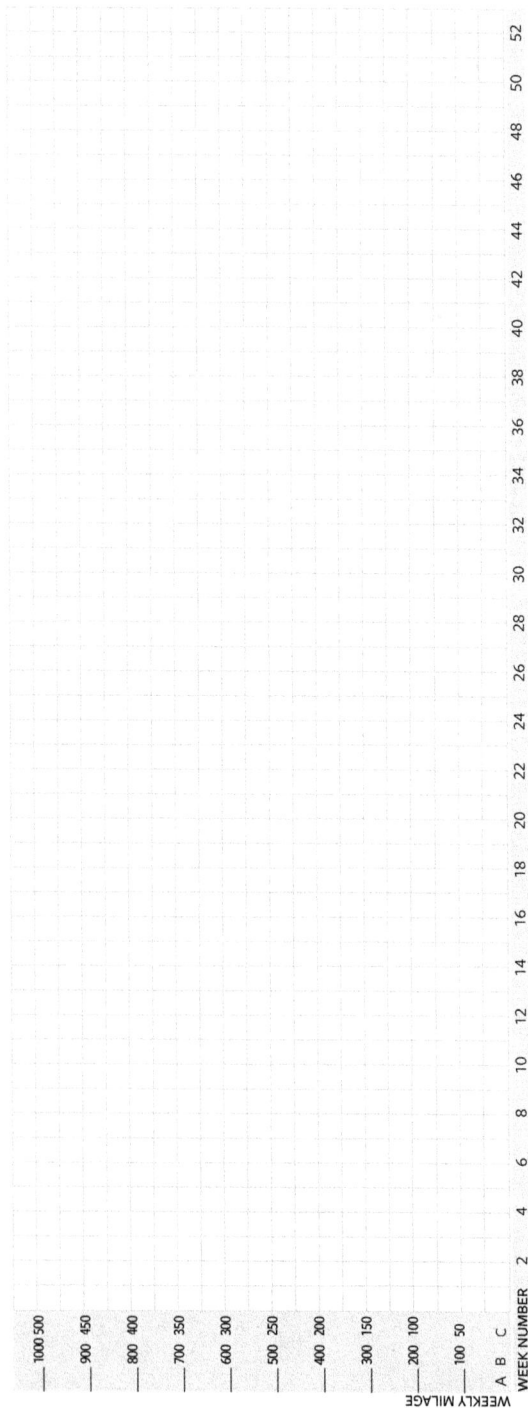

	A	B	C
	1000	500	
	900	450	
	800	400	
	700	350	
	600	300	
	500	250	
	400	200	
	300	150	
	200	100	
	100	50	

WEEKLY MILEAGE

WEEK NUMBER: 2 4 6 8 10 12 14 16 18 20 22 24 26 28 30 32 34 36 38 40 42 44 46 48 50 52

ACKNOWLEDGMENTS

The idea for this book was born one day after a conversation with my agent, Cynthia Ruchti. I set out to write a very different book—a book I still hope to write one day—but Cynthia suggested I write a book about running. Although Cynthia is not a runner and has struggled with knee issues, she said she was inspired by the reflections I was posting on Facebook after my runs.

My husband, Shawn, and I began to brainstorm. Shawn admitted that one of the goals on his dream list was to write a book. What would it look like if we crafted a book together? I offered up my devotional reflections. Shawn added his coaching tips and workouts, as well as his keen editing eye. Together and separately we logged hundreds of miles. That's how *Walk, Run, Soar* took flight.

Of course, as with any book project, a whole village of friends and family truly helped us build this content and championed us to the finish line.

Let's kick this party off by thanking Cynthia Ruchti, who is more than my agent. She's a prayer warrior, a word weaver, a cheerleader, and a mentor-friend. You have made this book even better with your non-runner insights and creative approach.

Jennifer Dukes Lee, you were an (in)courage sister-writer-friend first before you became my editor. Thank you for saying yes to this project and for sharing your family's own "walk, run, soar" story with us. We are deeply grateful for your loving prayers over our manuscript and your commitment to excellence in publishing.

To my late husband, Ericlee—You continue to encourage me with your loud coaching voice from heaven. Thank you for running your race well and leaving a legacy for all of us to chase after. You beat me to the finish, but I will meet you in Glory one day.

To my husband-coach, Shawn—You were my writing partner and first-draft editor. I'm so thankful you ran down the aisle with me on January 16, 2016, and said yes to stepping into this wild glory story. Thank you for leading our family well, processing all the minute details of the book with me, and wading through all those endnotes on our crazy road trip home from the Pacific Northwest.

To my oldest girl, Meilani—Thank you for helping your sisters along on all those early mornings when Mama was writing. I love seeing God grow your gifts of administration, leadership, and encouragement!

To my middle girl, Giada—Thank you for being my running buddy in this season of life, for leading your friends to pray for me along the way, and for carrying the Gilmore baton. Your resilience, perseverance, and compassion always inspire me.

To my youngest girl, Zayla—Thank you for your patience when Mama was trying to juggle all the things. You were my cutest and best cheerleader for this race! Thanks for your gift of music and enthusiasm, pushing me along.

To my mama, Maria—You have always been my biggest fan from my very first race to today. Thank you for your consistent prayers and extra time with the girls while I was stringing together words and chasing deadlines.

To my daddy, Doug—Thank you for taking me running for the first time all those years ago. From the Ridge Run to the Two Cities Half Marathon, from the graveside to the altar, you have been right by my side. Grateful for your example!

To my sister and brother-in-law, Caron and Rusty—It's my joy to have you joining the ranks in our running family. Thank you for cheering me on from the sidelines, through text messages, and running alongside me in this race!

To my brother and sister-in-law, Paul and Michelle—I'm so blessed to have you on my team. Thank you for all the fun running adventures and for sharing our words with your people.

To my in-laws, Christene and Larry—Thank you for believing in me and making space for me to write and travel by watching the girls.

To my Mama Florence, Cindy, Derek, and kids—What a gift to be grafted into your family and to share this love of running with all of you!

To my courageous friend and confidante, Yazmin—Thank you for walking this entire journey with me! You have been a safe place to process. Grateful for the ways you enter in, listen for God's leading, and sharpen me.

To my high school track coach, Tony Churchill—Thank you for calling me out to run for His glory and for championing me through the years. Your spiritual investment continues to bear fruit today!

To my Chai sisters, Amy, Terry, Yasmin, and Carla—You are home to me. I'm deeply thankful for all our conversations over Indian food and never-ending teacups of chai. Thank you for being in my corner!

To Whitney, Beth, Melissa, Sybil, Aly, Katie, and Jen—Thank you for always being just a text and a prayer away. You spur me on to love and good deeds with your leadership and truth-telling.

To Stephanie Bryant—Thank you for all the hours of Voxer chats. You empowered me with your words of affirmation, GIFs, gifts, any-time-of-the-day prayers, and cheerleading. So grateful for the ways our lives have connected even across the miles.

To all my (in)courage sisters, especially Becky, Tasha, Michelle, Grace, Alia, Dawn, Robin, Lucretia, Mary, Kaitlyn, and Holley—Thank you for faithfully checking in on me and offering up Instagram support and brainstorming on the publishing trail.

To my Pomegranate girls, Susan, Christine, Mary, Danna, and Stacie—Oh, how I love all our crazy Marco Polo chats! Thank you for running this race through the decades with Shawn and me.

To my Sunday life group friends, the Fords, Vasquezes, Willeys, Schmidts, and Benedicts—You are my people. Thank you for showing interest in the play-by-play of this journey.

To my Widow Mama Collective friends, especially Tara, Becky, and Lisa—I'm so grateful you were willing to partner with me and cheer me on in this project.

To the Moms in Christ at Fresno Christian Schools—You were my guinea pigs, listening intently to all my raw material. What a gift to join hands with you weekly!

To James Garcia and all our athletes at Fresno Christian Schools—You helped provide stories and ideas for this devotional—maybe without even knowing. Keep running your race for His glory!

To my mama-coaching friends, Kristi and Michele—I will treasure all our time together, cheering our kids on at running events and running together. Thank you for being faithful friends who show up in all seasons!

To all our running friends at Fleet Feet Fresno, San Joaquin Trail Runners, Sierra Challenge Express, and the Blue Badgers—We believe in the power of community. We loved being out on the trails and road with so many of you for races and training!

To the Go Mama Runners, especially my running buddies Katie, Stephanie, Amber, Heather, Esther, Marcy, Tanya, Kym, Johanna, and Marina—Thank you for pacing with me for all those dark o'clock miles and hills. You are warriors! I treasure our conversations and sisterhood.

To our Remember Haiti running team—You showed up every fall to train and raise money for projects in Haiti. This book was written for you. You helped us develop our coaching over the years, and you will recognize yourselves in many of these stories.

To my Hopewriter friends, especially the HW Authors Connect ladies, my hope circles, Emily Allen, Gloryanna Boge, Michelle

Diercks, Emily P. Freeman, Gary Morland, and Brian Dixon—You have provided a pathway to publishing. Thank you for your consistent message of hope and reminder to serve my reader!

To the Redbud Writers tribe—I can't thank you enough for helping me on this journey to publication. Thank you for linking arms and helping me build my audience and for sharing all your tips!

To my Bible study friends at the Well Community Church—Thank you for sharing my excitement in the process and lifting me up in prayer.

To Brad Bell, Melissa Danisi, Pattie Krohn, and all the pastors at The Well—Your preaching, teaching, and solid theology have certainly provided a foundation for me as these devotionals all came together.

To Mitchel Lee—Your sermons and example continue to inspire us from afar. Thank you for not forgetting to use the running metaphor!

NOTES

Chapter 19 Building Spiritual Muscles

1. Gretchen Reynolds, "Why lifting weights can be so potent for aging well," *New York Times*, March 20, 2019, https://www.nytimes.com/2019/03/20/well/move/lifting-weights-exercise-older-aging-muscles-psychology.html.

Chapter 25 Friend and Forerunner

1. Sara Holt, "Usain Bolt: The greatest athlete of all time?" CNN, August 19, 2016, https://www.cnn.com/2016/08/19/sport/usain-bolt-rio-2016-olympics-legacy/index.html.

Chapter 30 Honoring Our Sacred Bodies

1. Maria Furlough, *Confident Moms, Confident Daughters* (Grand Rapids: Revell, 2019), 18.

Chapter 36 Running to Worship

1. Eric Liddell quote from *Chariots of Fire*, directed by Hugh Hudson, written by Colin Welland, Allied Stars Ltd., 1981.
2. Eric Liddell in *Chariots of Fire*.

Chapter 49 Resting as Part of Training

1. Saundra Dalton-Smith, *Sacred Rest: Recover Your Life, Renew Your Energy, Restore Your Sanity* (Nashville: FaithWords, 2017).
2. Dorothy Kelley Patterson, *The Study Bible for Women* (Nashville: Holman Bible Publishers, 2014).

Dorina Gilmore Young is a writer, speaker, former news reporter, and longtime runner. She blogs at www.dorinagilmore.com and is a contributor on DaySpring's (in)courage writing team. She also writes regularly for the MOPS Blog and Kindred Mom. A widow, Dorina helps women through grief recovery. She remarried in 2016 to marathoner and triathlete Shawn Young, who provides the practical running tips in *Walk, Run, Soar*. Together, the Youngs coach cross-country and track teams. They live in California, raising three daughters to love the cultural diversity, beautiful landscapes, and unique food of the state.

www.ingramcontent.com/pod-product-compliance
Lightning Source LLC
Chambersburg PA
CBHW060753100426
42813CB00004B/799